101 WEEKENDS IN EUROPE

ROBIN BARTON

NEW
HOLLAND

Reprinted in 2013

This edition first published in 2008 by New Holland Publishers (UK) Ltd

London • Cape Town • Sydney • Auckland

www.newhollandpublishers.com

Garfield House, 86–88 Edgware Road, London, W2 2EA, United Kingdom

80 McKenzie Street, Cape Town, 8001, South Africa

Unit 1, 66 Gibbes Street, Chatswood, NSW 2067, Australia

218 Lake Road, Northcote, Auckland, New Zealand

ISBN 978 1 84773 081 7

Although the publishers have made every effort to ensure that information contained in this book was meticulously researched and correct at the time of going to press, they accept no responsibility for any inaccuracies, loss, injury or inconvenience sustained by any person using this book as reference.

Publisher: Ross Hilton
Copy Editor/Picture Research: Kelly Pipes
Designer: Roland Codd
Cartographer: Lovell Johns Limited
Senior Production Controller: Marion Storz

Reproduction by Modern Age Repro House Ltd, Hong Kong
Printed and bound by Times Offset (M) Sdn Bhd, Malaysia
10 9

PHOTOGRAPHY CREDITS

Front cover: © Grand Tour/Corbis; Back cover: © Pictures Colour Library (left, middle, right); Flaps: © Michelle Robek/Fotolia (right), © Dariusz Bajak/Fotolia (left); p1 © Anna Bryukhanova/IStockphoto; p2 © Tourismus Salzburg; p8 © Bertrand Gardel/Hemis /Corbis; p10 © Lars Endel / Alamy; p11 © Jenny Rollo; p12 © Saltzburg Tourist Information; p13 © Augenblicke/Fotolia; p14 © Marco Cristofori/Corbis; p16 © Visit Belgium; p17 © Jonathan Addie/Fotolia; p18 © Stan Rippel/Istockphoto; p20 © Vassil Donev/epa/Corbis; p22 © Tom Ang/Fotolia; p23 © Jelena Popic/Fotolia; p25 © Jaroslav Machacek/Fotolia; p26 © Michelle Robek/Fotolia; p27 © skvoor/Fotolia; p29 © Einar Bog/Fotolia; p30 © Lennart/Fotolia; p32 p© Andrei Nekrassov/Fotolia; p33 © Lev Dolgatshjov/Fotolia; p35 © Jon Sparks/Corbis; p37 © Frédéric/Fotolia; p38 © Chris Warren/PCL; p39 © Simon Heaton; p40 © David Noble/PCL; p41 © Gérard Defay/ Fotolia; p42 © JavierGil; p43 © David Noble; p44 © Jean-Michel Leclercq; p45 © Graham Lawrence/PCL; p46 © Guy Marchand/Fotolia; p47 © Jose Fuste Raga/Corbis; p48 © Atlantide Phototravel/Corbis; p49 © Xavier Horville/Fotolia; p51 © Brian Lawrence Images Ltd/PCL; p53 © Tom Davison/Fotolia; p54 © Jean-Michel Ducasse/Fotoia; p55 © Emmanuelle Bessez/Fotolia; p57 © Brian Lawrence Images Ltd/PCL; p58 © Downer/Fotolia; p59 © Matthew Whittle/Scanstockphoto; p60 © Brian Lawrence Images Ltd/Pictures Colour Library; p61 © Dagmar Schneider/Scanstockphoto; p62 © Stanley Rippel/Fotolia; p63 © DeVlce/Fotolia; p64 © Fabian Klenk/Fotolia; p66 © Sergio Cattivelli/scanstockphoto; p69 © laTresca/Fotolia; p71 © Jeremy Hoare/PCL; p72 © Lisa Vanovitch/scanstockphoto; p75 © Stephen L Saks/PCL; p75 © GeirHval/ scanstockphoto; p77 © Gary Nugent/scansctockphoto; p79 © Clive Sawyer/PCL; p80 © Sergio Pintaudi/Fotolia; p81 © Clive Sawyer/Pictures Colour Library; p82 © Adam Eastland/Pictures Colour Library; p83 © Stanislav Bratus/Fotolia; p84 © Picture Finders/PCL; p85 © Edmund Nagele/Pictures Colour Library; p86 © Stéphanie Marassoglou/Fotolia; p87 © Doug Pearson/JAI/Corbis; p88 © David Barnes/PCL; p89 © Adam Eastland/PCL; p90 © Marek Slusarczyk/PCL; p91 © RJ Lerich/PCL; p92 © iStockphoto.com/Marco Prandina; p93 © MajusС00L/Fotolia; p94 © Ted Levine/ zefa/Corbis; p96 © AJE/Fotolia; p98 © Mantas/Fotolia; p100 © AnnTriling/ scanstockphoto; p102 © Brian Lawrence Images Ltd/PCL; p103 © Minitchii/Fotolia; p104 © Jan Kranendonk; p106 © Brian Lawrence Images Ltd/PCL; p107 © John/Fotolia; p109 © Magdalena Majer/Fotolia; p110 © Alexander van Deursen/Fotolia; p111 © Tomasz Kubis/Fotolia; p112 © Vantime/Fotolia; p114 © Monica Wells/PCL; p115 © Rui Vale de Sousa/Fotolia; p117 © Monica Wells/PCL; p119 © alexford/Fotolia; p121 © foto.fritz/Fotolia; p123 © Ian O'Hanlon/Fotolia; p125 © Turespaña; p126 © Turespaña; p127 © Turespaña; p128 © Kjell Varin/Scanstockphoto; p129 © Robert Paul van Beets/Fotolia; p130 © Elin Saetersdal/Scanstockphoto; p131 © Cala Xarraca/PCL; p132 © Grzegorz Lepiarz/Istockphoto; p133 © J.D. Dallet/PCL; p134 © Inter Vision Ltd/Pictures Colour Library; p135 © Edmund Nagele/PCL; p136 © Johannes Norpoth/Istockphoto; p137 © Freefly/Fotolia; p140 © Benjamin So/Istockphoto; p141 © Elisa Locci/scanstockphoto; p142 © Mikael Lindstam/Scanstockphoto; p143 © Mikael Damkier/Istockphoto; p145 © Moritz Frei/Fotolia; p146 © Bertrand Rieger/Hemis/Corbis; p147 © Geir Olav Lyngfjell/Scanstcokphoto; p148 © Gustavo Fadel/scanstockphoto; p150 © Picture Finders/Pictures Colour Library; p152 © Belfast Tourism; p153 © Andres Rodriguez/scanstockphoto; p154 © Gail Johnson/Fotolia; p155 © Ai-Lan Lee/Fotolia; p156 © Edmund Nagele/Pictures Colour Library; p157 © photgl/Fotolia; p158 © Graham Lawrence/Pictures Colour Library; p159 © Charles Bowman/PCL; p160 © Jane Songhurst/Fotolia.

CONTENTS

YOUR NEXT 101 WEEKENDS IN EUROPE

As the muezzin's dawn chorus rings out across Istanbul from the city's Blue Mosque, summoning the faithful to prayer, just two hours and 2, 414 kilometres (1,500 miles) away London's nightlife is in full swing and Parisian bakers will soon be rolling the day's first croissants. Europe might be dwarfed by other continents but what it lacks in size it makes up for in diversity, depth and history.

From the Italian Renaissance to the Industrial Revolution, Europe has shaped the modern world. But it hasn't neglected the little pleasures in life such as chocolate, whisky and perfume. Whatever your passion, somewhere in Europe you can feed it.

In the last ten years, our travel habits have changed profoundly. Short on time, hungry for new experiences, we have embraced the long weekend break. The boom of the internet and the European Open Skies Treaty created ideal conditions for low-cost air travel. No longer did you have to book an expensive flight to a national hub and then travel onward, now you could fly direct to cities like Seville, Tallinn or Naples. Today, about 70 low-cost airlines operate across Europe, from Scandinavia to Spain. Most sell electronic tickets (e-tickets) over the internet, with prices varying according to demand. Train travel has also pressed the fast-forward button with high-speed links between European cities becoming much more widespread.

The purpose of this book is to help you plan your next weekend in Europe, and the next and the next... It will spark ideas, champion some of Europe's less obvious destinations – Leipzig, Bologna, Bergen and others – and suggest new ways of experiencing old favourites. Organised by country, 101 of the most memorable weekend destinations are described. Some European regions are accessed by little-known airports, such as the Dordogne (Bergerac), Umbria (Perugia), Puglia (Brindisi), The Loire (Angers). These places are listed under the gateway city. Where a destination majors in a particular area – such as food, culture, sightseeing or adventure – I've suggested special itineraries. Nowhere else rewards unscripted travel quite like Europe. World-famous sights – the Colosseum, the Alhambra, the Eiffel Tower – might hog the limelight but the most magical experiences are often found in the out-of-the-way places: the perfect *moules frites* in a Belgian café, the shimmer of the aurora borealis above Reykjavik or a balmy, Christmas-time stroll along Palma's seafront past palm trees garlanded with lights.

Of Europe's 48 countries, 27 are members of the European Union (the EU), a post-war, pan-European group of governments working towards common economic and political goals. Recent admissions to this controversial club include Bulgaria and Romania in 2007, while Macedonia, Croatia and Turkey are candidate countries. The EU's single currency, the euro, is used by half the member states. Border controls are minimal in the EU and sources of further information have been listed.

Like the best tapas, the beauty of weekending in Europe is that it always leaves you wanting more, another quick hit of pleasure. If you don't like somewhere, well, you can always laugh about it at work on Monday. But if you get woken at 5am by the wail of the muezzin in Istanbul, don't say you weren't warned.

Low-cost Airlines Versus Standard Airlines

Budget air travel can mean making a few compromises. Here are the ways that low-cost airlines differ from the traditional, national carriers.

- Stricter baggage restrictions – you may not be allowed as large a free allowance and you may have to pay to check in luggage
- Tighter ticket restrictions – it may be impossible or expensive to change or amend tickets
- Check-in times are tightly policed
- The destination's airport may not be a city's main airport but a smaller airport further from the city centre
- No free in-flight snacks or meals
- The ticket may incur hidden fees and taxes

A Taste of Europe

- Most adventurous places – sailing Croatia's Adriatic coast, surfing the Atlantic at Biarritz, kite surfing at Tarifa in Andalucia, mountain biking in the Scottish Borders, laying first tracks at La Grave, off-road driving in Iceland
- Jaw-dropping sights – Cologne's cathedral, the Uffizi gallery in Florence, the Hermitage in St Petersburg, the Guggenheim in Bilbao, the Alhambra in Granada
- Where to find heavenly meals – Bologna, Brussels, Cork, Luxembourg, Lyon, Turin
- Musical nights out – a winter ball in Vienna, cabaret in Berlin, show-hopping in Edinburgh during the festival, open-air classical concerts in Budapest, pub gigs in Galway
- Europe's architects – Charles Rennie Mackintosh (Glasgow), Victor Horta (Brussels), Sir Norman Foster (London, Palma, Berlin), Daniel Libeskind (Berlin), Rem Koolhaas (Riga, Porto)
- Top for shops – Antwerp, Milan, Paris, London

Alexander III Bridge, Paris

101 WEEKENDS IN EUROPE

WHERE TO GO IF YOU LIKE...

FOOD...
Bruges
Brussels
Carcassonne
Luxembourg
Parma
Perugia

DRINK...
Bordeaux
Brussels
Jerez
Porto

MUSIC...
Budapest
Salzburg
Seville
Vienna

FESTIVALS...
Deauville
Edinburgh
Salzburg
Vienna

FASHION...
Antwerp
London
Milan
Paris

WINTER SPORTS...
Geneva
Grenoble
Innsbruck
Kiruna

WATER SPORTS...
Biarritz
Dubrovnik
Newquay
Split

ARCHITECTURE...
Antwerp
Copenhagen
Glasgow
Helsinki
Stockholm

ADVENTURE SPORTS...
Bergen
Klagenfurt
Ljubljana
Pau

ROMANCE...
Istanbul
Paris
Prague
Tallinn

ART...
Amsterdam
Basel
Bilbao
Copenhagen
Delft
Luxembourg
Paris
St Petersburg

NIGHTLIFE...
Barcelona
Berlin

Krakow
Lisbon

CAFÉ CULTURE...
Brno
Riga
Sofia
Vilnius

SIGHTSEEING...
Athens
Brno
Cologne
Copenhagen
Edinburgh
Granada
Krakow
Palma
Paris
Prague
Salzburg
Tallinn
Vienna
Wroclaw

Night time in Dubrovnik

AUSTRIA

Restrained, ordered and ever so slightly unfashionable; the Austrian stereotype couldn't be further from the truth. With a rich musical heritage, cities like Salzburg and Vienna also have hip quarters packed with bars and clubs. And while Austria's infrastructure may work with Teutonic efficiency, like one of legendary skier Herman Maier's downhill runs, when Austrians let their hair down they don't hold back. Austria's winter ski resorts may look quaint but the nightlife is, in most, as exciting as the skiing. Whether you're an outdoors lover or a fan of culture, architecture and slick city life, Austria can offer great weekends away whatever the time of year.

TIME DIFFERENCE GMT +1 (Central European Summer Time +2)

TELEPHONE CODE +43

CURRENCY Euro

LANGUAGE German

NATIONAL TRANSPORT WEBSITE www.oebb.at

POPULATION 8,300,000

SIZE OF COUNTRY 83,855 sq km (32,377 sq m)

CAPITAL Vienna

WHEN TO GO In winter, Austria is an alpine wonderland with ski resorts readily accessible from Innsbruck. The lower-lying cross-country skiing areas around Klagenfurt may have variable snow outside the mid-winter. Spring brings warm weather and sunshine; Klagenfurt becomes a hotbed of outdoor activities. Salzburg and Vienna are also year-round destinations with music festivals during the summer and charming markets at Christmas. Temperatures can get very high in mid-summer: the most pleasant months are April to the end of June and September to October.

TOURIST INFORMATION www.austria.info

001 INNSBRUCK

HOW TO GET THERE

British Airways has direct, early-morning flights to Innsbruck from London Gatwick twice a week. easyJet also fly to Innsbruck but at less convenient times.

CONTACTS/FURTHER INFORMATION

www.innsbruck-tourismus.at

High on the slopes above Mayrhofen ski resort

Is a weekend's skiing an unrealistic proposition? Only if you can't get on the slopes by lunchtime on the first day. There's no such problem at Innsbruck where early-bird flights leave the UK at 7am, meaning that a midday start is perfectly possible. The skiing at Innsbruck, one of the most well-rounded Austrian resorts, is centred on a handful of villages just a 20-minute drive from the city. Bigger, glitzier names – St. Anton and Kitzbühel – are an hour away by car but for a weekend you're better off getting to grips with

> "The **self-styled** Capital of the Alps is the **only** European city to offer world-class skiing"

slopes closer to your base such as Igls, site of an Olympic-standard bobsleigh track, and Seefeld, a village with extensive cross-country ski tracks. The low-key, laid-back Austrian resort of Mayrhofen is 40-minutes from Innsbruck and is perhaps the biggest draw for snow-seekers in the area. Boasting one of Europe's best fun parks, with 20-metre (66-feet) jumps sending boarders as high as the chairlift, Mayrhofen caters to skiers and boarders alike. It's a low-lying resort so expect the snow to vanish towards the end of the season, but it still offers the steepest piste in Austria: the Harakiri.

The self-styled capital of the Alps is the only European city to offer world-class skiing – it has twice hosted the Winter Olympics – and a hefty dose of culture. Even summer visitors will find plenty to do, apart from hiking in the surrounding mountains. The city's most notable sight is the Golden Roof, a three-story Tyrolean balcony in the heart of Innsbruck's medieval Old Town. It's not actually golden; the effect comes from the copper tiles. The balcony dates from the start of the 16th century and the surrounding buildings are similarly historic. The Golden Roof is pre-dated by the Imperial Palace, an impressive, Gothic palace that later had a baroque makeover. Nightlife can include evenings at the opera or dinner at restaurants that serve much more than that hearty staple of Austrian mountain life, *Tiroler grostl* (Tyrolean hash).

Of all the weekend skiing options available, the capital of the Tyrol perhaps makes the most sense.

HOW TO GET THERE
Ryanair fly to Klagenfurt from
London Stansted

**CONTACTS/FURTHER
INFORMATION**
www.info.klagenfurt.at

Lake Wörthersee

KLAGENFURT

Austria's rural southern province of Carinthia, bordering Slovenia and Italy, opened its doors to the outside world when Ryanair began a service from London Stansted to Klagenfurt, the regional capital. Carinthians (there are 550,000 of them) are surrounded by 1,270 lakes and several mountain ranges. With such a natural playground to hand, Carinthians take their sports very seriously. Visitors can take their pick from a huge choice of water sports: sailing, windsurfing and waterskiing on the vast lake Wörthersee, or scuba diving, kayaking, rafting and canyoning, which combines both water and mountains. The uncrowded, limestone canyons south of Klagenfurt on the border with Slovenia are made for exploring on foot – but canyoneers will need to wear a helmet and wetsuit plus some sticky-soled shoes. An equally thrilling way to get a taste of the outdoors is white-water rafting. For genuinely high-graded rafting you will need to head across the border into Slovenia to

tackle the raging Soca river, but family-friendly thrills are on offer on the River Moll and Drau in Carinthia.

From springtime onwards, the region's lakes become the focal point for weekends in the water. Wörthersee is the largest inland bathing area in Europe and the water, which is of drinking quality, quickly warms up to bathtub temperatures.

Even out of the water, this part of Austria is very much a weekend destination for active types. There are numerous hiking routes in the mountains, although Klagenfurt lies in a valley and you will have to travel up to resorts like the tiny Nassfeld. Summer sports including tennis, golf and cycling are all extremely well represented with dedicated courts, courses and cycle paths. The self-styled capital of sports is perfect if you need to let off some steam but sightseers might wish for more than the city's most popular attraction: MiniMundus, a collection of the world's most famous tourist attractions – in miniature.

003

HOW TO GET THERE
Salzburg is well served by low-cost airlines with Jet2, Ryanair, Flybe and Thomsonfly all departing UK airports for the city. Salzburg's airport is very close to the city.

CONTACTS/FURTHER INFORMATION
www.salzburg.info
www.museumdermoderne.at

Winter panorama of city

SALZBURG

July and August see Mozart's birthplace come alive with music. The annual Salzburg Festival is one of the world's great cultural occasions. The opera festival was founded in 1920 and now boasts an international repertoire of performers and directors. Over the years the main venue, an open-air theatre cut into cliffs, has expanded and is now named the House of Mozart. Don't be misled by the title, however, the month-long festival showcases music from composers old and new.

Salzburg's Altstadt, the Old Town, also known as the Left Bank, is on high ground overlooked by the Mönchsberg cliffs. You can take a lift to the top of the mountain for views over Salzburg and the River Salzach. Up here, the Museum of Modern Art exhibits post-war art and sculpture in a stunning modernist setting that can detract from the works on show. Making your way down to ground level again, you can continue the sightseeing by walking to St Rupert's cathedral, an Italianate church in Residenzplatz.

Salzburg is a compact and comfortably well-off city with parks, lakes and easy access to the mountainous countryside. Two of the city's parks are featured in *The Sound of Music*; Julie Andrews sang Do-Re-Mi in the Mirabell Gardens, and the gazebo in the Schlosspark just outside the city also makes an appearance. And with the mountains of northern Austria on Salzburg's doorstep it's no schlep for skiers to get to Schladming and other ski resorts.

Mozart

There's plenty of Mozart memorabilia in the souvenir shops but when it comes to sites associated with the composer, Salzburg doesn't go over the top. In 1756 the prodigy was born at 9 Getreidegasse, now the Geburtshaus, a museum with some early instruments of his. As a young adult Mozart lived at 8 Makartplatz and the museum here has a more detailed account of his life.

VIENNA

Mozart was born in Salzburg but it is clear where his affections lay: 'When I am in Salzburg I long for a hundred amusements but here not for a single one' he wrote to his father from Vienna. 'For just to be in Vienna is entertainment enough,' he concluded. Mozart's most successful years were undoubtedly those he spent in the Austrian capital. You can get a flavour of the art and music of Vienna in just a few days, although culture vultures should expect to make a return visit to do everything they missed first time round.

Vienna is organised rather like an onion, with the Old Town, the UNESCO-protected Innere Stadt, bordered by a series of ring roads on one side and the Danube to the northeast. Most of the key attractions are in the Innere Stadt and it is easy to navigate your way to the remainder; a tram service circles the inner ring road (the Ringstrasse) and you can jump off at any point. From this ring road you can get good views of old Vienna's neo-classical architecture.

Many things in central Vienna are expensive but not the sound of music. You can buy tickets to the Viennese State Opera on the day of performance at a very reasonable rate, if you're happy with standing room only. Tickets are also sold a month in advance online, which is another way of saving money. Theatres and concert halls abound in Vienna (there are three opera houses alone, although none match the splendour of the State Opera house) so there will be something on whenever you visit. Another sly way to hear music for free is to go to church on Sunday; the city's

HOW TO GET THERE
British Airways and Austrian Airlines fly to Vienna from London Heathrow. Note that many of the low-cost airlines, including easyJet and Ryanair fly to Bratislava airport – it is a 90-minute transfer to Vienna.

CONTACTS/FURTHER INFORMATION
www.vienna.info
www.staatsoper.at
www.vienneseball.org
www.schoenbrunn.at

State Opera house

darkly Gothic cathedral, the Stephansdom, has two morning masses.

This is a city fuelled by coffee and pastries and its cafés open for a very leisurely Sunday brunch. Afterwards you can walk off the calories in the gardens of the Schloss Schönbrunn, the city's baroque palace and one-time residence of the Habsburg royals.

Mozart is as celebrated in Vienna as he is in Salzburg: his apartment on Domgasse – apparently a whirlwind of riotous behaviour, as well as the setting for the composition of *The Marriage of Figaro* – is preserved as the Mozarthaus.

Genteel and sophisticated it may be, but Vienna also has an edgier underbelly most readily found along the Gurtel, an outer ring road below an elevated U-Bahn track. Attracted by low rents and a very un-Viennese cityscape, hip bars and clubs have sprung up around stations such as Nussdorferstrasse. Vienna also has a thriving electro music scene with DJs and producers ensuring that it is Central Europe's musical melting pot.

Viennese café

Waltz This Way

Viennese balls are legendary for their glamour but they are also surprisingly accessible, except perhaps the grande dame of the Viennese Ball season, the Vienna Opera Ball. Vienna's waltzing season starts on New Year's Eve with the Imperial Ball at the Hofburg and continues for three months in a uniquely European carnival of music and dancing. The Vienna Opera Ball takes place in the main auditorium of the Opera House on 31 January. Tickets are expensive and highly sought after, however one Austrian businessman has made it a life's mission to invite a different celebrity as his companion each year, ranging from Sophia Loren to Paris Hilton. Men wear white tie and tails and women a full-length ball gown – if you're not in the habit of attending balls a gown can be rented from several Viennese boutiques. Similarly, dance lessons are also widely available in the city (at the Elmayer Dancing School, for example) so you need not look like you have two left feet. The winter party season comes to a head with the colourful Fasching on Ash Wednesday when drunken revelry takes over from stately waltzing.

BELGIUM

Sandwiched between northern France and western Germany, Belgium has taken the best from both cultures to produce an exclusively Belgian take on food and drink. Belgian beer, its purity as rigorously guarded as beers in Germany, is perhaps the best in the world. Culinary classics such as *moules frites* are served in the many excellent restaurants in cities from Antwerp to Brussels. Belgium's hedonistic streak doesn't extend to sport – the favourite way of spending a drizzly Saturday morning in April is standing at a roadside to watch a passing cycling race. But sightseeing is altogether more rewarding with the picturesque city of Bruges topping the must-see list, while Antwerp pleases fashionistas.

TIME DIFFERENCE GMT +1 (Central European Summer Time +2)

TELEPHONE CODE +32

CURRENCY Euro

LANGUAGE Dutch and French

NATIONAL TRANSPORT WEBSITES
www.b-rail.be; www.eurostar.com

POPULATION 10,450,000

SIZE OF COUNTRY 30,520 sq km (11,784 sq m)

CAPITAL Brussels

WHEN TO GO Autumn and winter can be gloomy in Belgium, with cold temperatures and grey weather. Even spring can be variable. The best time for city breaks to Antwerp, Bruges and Brussels is May to September.

TOURIST INFORMATION www.visitbelgium.com

005 ANTWERP

HOW TO GET THERE
VLM Air flies to Antwerp from
London City and Manchester.

**CONTACTS/FURTHER
INFORMATION**
www.visitantwerp.be

City Hall

Diamonds might be forever but Antwerp is as famous for its fashion scene these days as it is for being the hub of Europe's diamond trading business. Belgian designers such as Ann Demeulemeester, Dirk Bikkemberg and Dries van Noten have cut out a distinctive corner of the fashion world, separate from Paris, Milan and London, in this Belgian city. Shopping for fashion is one of Antwerp's top attractions; make your way to Nationalestraat, Sint-Antoniusstraat and Kammenstraat for the independent outlets of Belgium's leading designers.

The source of this unique thread of Belgian fashion know-how goes back many centuries to when Flanders was at the heart of Europe's textile weaving industry. To make the most of the woven wool, the Antwerp Royal Academy of the Fine Arts was founded in 1663, which includes one of the toughest schools of fashion design in the world. The end of year show is one of the surest indicators of future talent. In 2002 the fabulous ModeMuseum opened and showcases Belgian fashions on Nationalestraat.

The city's artistic reputation doesn't just rest on the shoulders of its designers. The 17th-century painter Peter Paul Rubens lived and worked in Antwerp, teaching, among others, the artist Antony van Dyck. Antwerp's Gothic cathedral contains four works by Rubens while others are displayed in the Royal Museum of the Fine Arts.

Antwerp is also a colossal and wealthy seaport, straddling the River Scheldt, but its centre has retained many intriguing features, particularly in the Grote Markt part of the old town where 16th-century architecture still dazzles. The harbour side is being redeveloped with the arrival of trendy bars and restaurants; this is a city that enjoys a night out, preferably fuelled by the superb Belgian beers before you hit Antwerp's lounges and clubs. With so many fashionistas arriving in the city you can also expect some cutting-edge hotels in which to lay your head.

"In 2002 the fabulous **ModeMuseum** opened and showcases Belgian **fashions** on Nationalestraat."

HOW TO GET THERE
Direct trains from London to Brussels with Eurostar; flights with BMI, Flybe and British Airways from various UK airports.

CONTACT DETAILS/FURTHER INFORMATION
www.brusselsinternational.be

The Grand Place, Brussels

BRUSSELS

It takes a good sense of timing and direction to penetrate Brussels' ring road; but if you arrive by train rather than car, the journey couldn't be smoother. The Belgian capital has superb rail links with London, Paris and other European cities, as you might expect from a city that defines the modern European Union. The city is the home of the European Commission, NATO and the Council of the European Union. So, is it really any surprise, in a city peopled by politicians, that so many excellent restaurants abound? Brussels boasts a constellation of Michelin stars, with hundreds of brasseries and restaurants operating to a very high standard. *Moules frites* (mussels with french fries) is to Brussels what fish and chips is to England – except you stand a much better chance of getting a memorable meal in Brussels. The streets around the Grand Place are a good hunting ground for a plate of the freshest mussels. Although everyone should try the city speciality at least once, foodies will find themselves exploring menus with gusto for glimpses of Belgian culinary

genius such as rabbit stewed in beer.

And beer is another superb reason to spend the weekend in Brussels; 600 reasons in fact, as that is how many varieties are sold in bars throughout the city. Brussels alone makes 120 types of beer, typically strong, flavoursome and capable of putting any British brew to shame. Belgian beer's appeal lies in its variety: from frisky, hoppy ales to dark, winey stouts, there's something for every meal. With so many beers available, Belgians have an incentive to get the bars right too, and many of Brussels' best bars, such as the art deco L'Archiduc on Rue Antoine Dansaert, are wonderfully time-warped places.

Belgium fostered the art nouveau movement and Brussels' most pervasive architect, Victor Horta, created some beautifully coherent examples of the style that have aged well over the century. Horta's home is now a museum but you can also enjoy art nouveau architecture with a beer in your hand at the Mort Subite bar on Rue Montagne aux Herbes Potagères.

007

BRUGES

HOW TO GET THERE
Hop on a train from Brussels
or go via ferry to Dunkirk (from
Dover) with Norfolkline and
then drive north to Bruges.

**CONTACTS/FURTHER
INFORMATION**
www.brugge.be

*Colourful buildings on a
Bruges canal*

It's a fine line between preserving a medieval gem of a city and the disappointment of theme-park heritage: this gorgeous Flemish city stays just on the right side. The city's lofty gabled houses overlook placid canals now plied by sightseeing boats while horse-drawn carts rattle along the car-free cobbled streets. There are few must-see museums but Bruges' status as an extremely popular city break is based on two factors: the wonderfully pretty streets to roam and the highest concentration of chocolatiers in Europe.

Belgian chocolate is one of life's most pleasurable indulgences and there are about 50 shops in central Bruges where you can taste a little piece of heaven. Try one of the 60 varieties at the Chocolate Line shop on Simon Stevinplein, founded by Dominique Persoone, the self-styled 'shock-o-latier'. Many of the shops are covered by the Chocolate Walks, a map sold by the tourist office that also entitles you to free tastings. If you're still mad about the cocoa bean, there is a Chocolate Museum and an annual Chocolate Festival in April.

Bruges' roots lie in the Flemish aptitude for trade; Belgium has access to the sea and a position at the heart of Europe, so for centuries trade, particularly in Flemish cloth, flourished. Bruges' affluence can be seen in the grand merchants' houses all around the city and the imposing civic buildings surrounding the vast Market Square. No modern buildings intrude here. The Town Hall is a masterpiece of Gothic architecture; the ceiling of the dazzling Gothic Room dates from 1402 and paintings found here illustrate Bruges' lucrative past. The city centre is very compact and can be covered on foot in half an hour; if you arrive by car, park at one of the underground car parks on the edge of the centre.

BULGARIA

Bulgaria is slowly transforming itself from a post-Communist state to a modern democracy; it joined the EU in January 2007, 17 years after its Communist leaders were ousted. This large country in the far east of Europe, south of Romania, has much in its favour. The capital, Sofia, is a rapidly modernising city with some stunning sights. Sofia is the gateway for most international travellers, many of whom continue to the Black Sea beach resorts to the east. However, weekenders should explore Sofia's environs, particularly the rugged mountain ranges to the south.

TIME DIFFERENCE GMT +2 (Eastern European Summer Time +3)

TELEPHONE CODE +359

CURRENCY Lev

LANGUAGE Bulgarian

NATIONAL TRANSPORT WEBSITE www.bdz.bg

POPULATION 7,600,000

SIZE OF COUNTRY 110,994 sq km (42,855 sq m)

CAPITAL Sofia

WHEN TO GO Temperatures can rocket skyward in the summer, so if you are planning to sightsee go in May/June or September/October to avoid heatwave conditions. Winters can be mild but snow does fall at higher levels, at the ski resorts.

TOURIST INFORMATION www.bulgariatravel.org

008

HOW TO GET THERE
Bulgaria Air, Mytravel and
Thomas Cook Airlines all fly to
Sofia from London Gatwick.

**CONTACTS/FURTHER
INFORMATION**
www.bulgariatourism.org

*Rainbow over Aleksandr Nevsky
Cathedral*

SOFIA

Stationed at the frontier of Europe, bordering Greece, Turkey, Romania, Serbia and the Black Sea, eastern and western cultures have long mixed in Bulgaria. In the cosmopolitan capital city, Sofia, you'll find ancient Russian churches, one of the largest synagogues in Europe and a 16th-century Ottoman mosque. Even the Communists left a legacy of a handful of handsome administrative buildings.

The people too are similarly diverse, although they share a typically Bulgarian friendliness, giving visitors to their country a warm welcome. And there's a lot for visitors to enjoy here. You can combine a Black Sea beach break with culture by visiting Varna, the most stylish city on the Black Sea coast and home to the remarkable Archaeological Museum and the third largest Roman baths in Europe.

Sofia's compact historic centre merits exploration, although the cafés lining the wide, clean pavements may prove to be a tempting distraction even from the breathtaking Aleksandr Nevsky Cathedral and the atmospheric Sveta Nedelya Cathedral.

Bulgarian cuisine relies on fresh vegetables such as cucumbers, sweet peppers and tomatoes so don't worry – however much you eat, it's still healthy. Dishes, such as stuffed and roast red peppers or homemade cheeses, are typically simple but delicious. Wine lovers will discover that the same is true of Bulgarian wines; they may be cheap, but that doesn't mean you shouldn't expect some seriously good bottles.

One of the undisputed highlights of Bulgaria is Rila Monastery, high in the Rila Mountains, the closest range to Sofia and due south of the city. The monastery has UNESCO status and attracts thousands of Bulgarians and foreigners alike to its stunning setting and preserved frescoes. The monastery is at the foot of Mt Malyovitsa, the birthplace of Bulgarian climbing. The snow-capped, 2,729-metre (8,953-feet) peak was first climbed in 1938 by a pair of Bulgarian climbers, although trekking is a more common way of ascending the mountain these days. Rough, granite walls, lined with free climbing routes pepper the Malyovitsa region and the views from their summits make the effort worthwhile.

" **Dishes, such as stuffed and roast red peppers or homemade cheeses, are typically simple but delicious.** "

CROATIA

After the break-up of Yugoslavia, Croatia made the best of the hand it was dealt and in 2003 it applied to join the EU. Benefiting from a gorgeous Adriatic coastline where thousands of islands are surrounded by clean, clear waters, tourism has become a major industry. The handsome, historic city of Dubrovnik is the centre for sightseers in the southern tip of the country, while Split is the jumping-off point for sailing holidays around the islands of Hvar and Korcula. Whether you're a dedicated sun-seeker, a sailing obsessive or history buff, few places offer such a mesmerising combination of history and scenery.

TIME DIFFERENCE GMT +1 (Central European Summer Time +2)

TELEPHONE CODE +385

CURRENCY Kuna

LANGUAGE Croatian

NATIONAL TRANSPORT WEBSITE www.hznet.hr

POPULATION 4,500,000

SIZE OF COUNTRY 56,538 sq km (21,829 sq m)

CAPITAL Zagreb

WHEN TO GO Croatia is predominantly a summer destination: go in the peak of summer to enjoy various water sports but prepare for accommodation and activities to be crowded. June and September are particularly good months to go.

TOURIST INFORMATION www.croatia.hr

HOW TO GET THERE
Flybe (from Birmingham) and
Thomsonfly have direct
services to Dubrovnik (from
Manchester and Gatwick).

**CONTACTS/FURTHER
INFORMATION**
www.tzdubrovnik.hr
www.rya.org.uk
www.neilson.co.uk

Old Town

DUBROVNIK

Since the break-up of Yugoslavia in the 1990s and the cessation of hostilities, Dubrovnik has become a highly sought-after city break. Although Dubrovnik was shelled during the conflict, the Croatian port's beauty is undeniable; it must be one of the most well-preserved medieval towns in Europe. But its new-found popularity means that during the summer holidays it is crammed with visitors disgorged from cruise ships and airplanes. To enjoy Dubrovnik at its best, arrive in May or September.

Three city gates allow entry into Dubrovnik's golden heart, a warren of weathered, limestone buildings where staircases lead into ever tighter alleyways and under ancient arches. The main street, Stradun (or Placa), running east to west, was in flames in 1991. Today the street is lined with shops but previously it connected the massive defensive sea walls – which you can walk – with the administrative side of the city.

Dubrovnik is staking a claim to be the new Riviera of the Med, with summer festivals and ever more luxurious hotels, although it is still good value. But you can escape the throng by heading to Mljet Island, a national park, or simply weighing anchor in a yacht.

Sailing in the Adriatic

With more than 1,000 islands anchored in crystal clear seas, the Dalmatian coast of Croatia is one of the most beautiful sailing destinations in the world. Whether you're an old sea dog or a first-timer, there will be facilities ready for you. For experienced sailors with appropriate RYA (Royal Yachting Association) qualifications, 'bare boating' – renting a yacht without a skipper – is an option. Those after a more relaxing break can charter a yacht with a crew and a captain; the amount of work you do is up to you. And for those who have never tacked or reached, there are two RYA-approved schools in the area, one run by international travel company Neilson and the other close to Split.

SPLIT

The Dalmatian capital is two-thirds of the way down Croatia's Adriatic coast, north of Dubrovnik. While not as overwhelmingly beautiful as Dubrovnik, Split is a gorgeously sun-kissed place to spend the weekend, with opportunities to explore some of the wonderful islands off Croatia's craggy coast. Hvar island, for example, is a new playground of the Euro glitterati.

Split was founded by the Roman emperor Diocletian; the city was to be his retirement paradise and his palace was completed in AD 305. The ruins of the palace can still be seen in the centre of Split and the entire complex is protected by UNESCO World Heritage status today, although that hasn't stopped locals setting up shop there since the 6th century. You can get great views over the city and the palace from the Marjan Forest Park.

Split is the cultural heart of Croatia, with an important summer festival and several theatre groups. During the summer it is easy to find live music or performance then continue the evening at one of the bars behind Bacvice beach, where the hottest nightlife can be found. The restaurant quarter is in neighbouring Firula. For most people, Split is simply a transit point for onward journeys to the Dalmatian islands, but new hotels and restaurants are encouraging people to stay for longer.

Hvar

A short ferry journey from Split, Hvar island is one of the most fashionable places in Croatia. It's a yachtie haven and the island's town, Hvar, ranks alongside Dubrovnik for attractiveness; like Dubrovnik, Hvar has strong Venetian influences, having been ruled by Venice until 1700. The town's centre is a resplendent square surrounded by Renaissance palaces, a cathedral and a small harbour of fishing boats. Around this harbour are hundreds of waterfront cafés and bars plus some upmarket restaurants. The island is the sunniest place in Croatia and there's no better way to spend the day than soaking up the rays while watching the world go by in the harbour. The interior of the island is a fragrant oasis of wild herbs and olive trees.

HOW TO GET THERE
Flybe (from Birmingham) and Thomsonfly (from London Gatwick) have direct flights to Split.

CONTACTS/FURTHER INFORMATION
www.visitsplit.com
www.hvar.hr

Yachts in Split harbour

CZECH REPUBLIC

TIME DIFFERENCE GMT +1 (Central European Summer Time +2)

TELEPHONE CODE +420

CURRENCY Koruna

LANGUAGE Czech

NATIONAL TRANSPORT WEBSITE www.cd.cz

POPULATION 10,300,000

SIZE OF COUNTRY 178,864 sq km (30,450 sq m)

CAPITAL Prague

WHEN TO GO Much of the Czech Republic closes in winter although it can be a good time to visit Prague without the crowds. Otherwise, May to September is the main tourist season.

TOURIST INFORMATION www.czechtourism.com

When low-cost airlines began their foray into the European mainland, Prague bore the brunt of the assault. But look beyond the cheap, delicious beer of the Czech Republic and you'll find a country with a strong, proud artistic heritage and an enviable architectural backdrop featuring marvellous art nouveau and baroque buildings. Brno, the Czech Republic's second city, is a pleasant, low-key alternative to the capital Prague. Both cities, however, offer the kind of free-wheeling revelry that would have been unimaginable prior to the Velvet Revolution of 1989 when the Communist rulers relinquished control of the country.

HOW TO GET THERE
Ryanair flies to Brno from
London Stansted.

**CONTACTS/FURTHER
INFORMATION**
www.brno.cz
www.spilberk.cz

*Cathedral of St Peter
and Paul*

BRNO

The Czech Republic's second city is an understated understudy to the headline act, Prague, but it carries off its role with style. It has a small but condensed city centre with some wonderfully baroque buildings and an olde-worlde atmosphere, thanks to the trams that rattle up and down the streets. Brno was a cornerstone of the Habsburg Empire when the rule of the Austro-Hungarian family extended over what was then Bohemia. You can get a feel for the Habsburg's rule by visiting the Spilberk Castle, which was one prison you didn't want to be sent to in the 18th and 19th centuries: the castle dungeons were a setting for torture. During the Nazi occupation the castle became a Gestapo-run prison. Today it hosts exhibitions and festivals but it hasn't lost its grim and foreboding aspect.

After a visit to Spilberk, a stroll around the city centre will raise the mood. Brno has far fewer tourists than Prague but the beer flows just as freely in the bars and food in the restaurants is cheap and filling. This is also a university city with a vibrant nightlife and a busy summer season of arts and music festivals.

Milan Kundera

Prague is famous for being the home of novelist Franz Kafka but it is not so well known that Brno also has a writer of its own: Milan Kundera, best-known for *The Unbearable Lightness of Being*. Kundera was born in Brno in 1929 and studied in the city before joining Prague's Academy of Performing Arts as a lecturer. It was in Prague that Kundera got to know key figures in the Prague Spring of 1968 and the Velvet Revolution, such as Vaclav Havel. Although a member of the Czechoslovakian Communist Party, Kundera was blacklisted by the organisation and he escaped to France.

012 PRAGUE

HOW TO GET THERE
BMI, easyJet, Jet2 and British Airways all have regular services from various UK airports to Prague.

CONTACTS/FURTHER INFORMATION
www.pis.cz
www.pivnigalerie.cz
www.chodovar.cz

Charles Bridge

With the opening of a Mandarin Oriental hotel in 2007, a branch of the Four Seasons and the surreally extravagant Hotel Yasmin just steps away from Wenceslas Square, Prague bears little resemblance to the austere years of Communism pre-1989. Prague's convoluted history – it has been occupied by French, German, Soviet and Prussian armies – took another twist after the peaceful Velvet Revolution of 1989 and by 1993 the city was the capital of the newly-formed Czech Republic. It surged into the new decade and quickly became one of Europe's most popular city breaks and almost a byword for stag party excesses. Fortunately the stag parties are moving onto even cheaper East European cities (Tallinn and Budapest among others) but Prague remains an affordable and beautiful place to visit. The old town has been a UNESCO World Heritage Site since 1992 and in the years following the Velvet Revolution the city centre seemed like a period film set: the faded glory of this capital of Bohemia was intoxicating and a night promenading along the riverside or across the ancient bridges over the River Vltava matched Paris or Venice for romance. You would settle down in a basic streetside restaurant or café with a plate of something stodgy and meaty (no haute cuisine here, and always order beer rather than wine). In short, it would be magical.

Times change. There's no Starbucks (yet) but there are branches of McDonalds in Prague now. In the peak season you may be jostled by camera-wielding sightseers as you cross the stone bridges or queue outside the best sights. But there's a solution. Prague is at its best out of season. During autumn, winter and early spring, Prague returns to those glorious post-revolution days. You can get a table in the best cafés, such as Café Slavia, the renovated Café Savoy or the Grand Café Orient in the surprisingly interesting Museum of Czech Cubism. And those heavy stews and dumplings finally make sense after a chilly day out. Beer-wise, in the winter you should turn your attention to the stronger, darker bocks

that the Czech brewers are starting to produce. Out of season you also stand a good chance of enjoying Prague's still-superb sights. The Old Town neighbourhoods of Stare Mesto and Male Strana, joined by the famous Charles Bridge, remain untouched by time. From the bridge you will be able to see Prague Castle against a probably cloudy-grey sky; it is one of the world's largest castles and dates from the 9th century. Inside are the crown jewels of the monarchs of Bohemia but you don't have to enter the castle to appreciate its grandeur – the floodlit courtyards are open until 11pm. Also part of the same complex, the St Vitus cathedral is a gorgeous Gothic construction, resembling a smaller version of Cologne's twin-towered Dom Cathedral. Another enchanting church worth a visit is that of St Nicholas – but you do have to go inside to get the full effect of the extravagant decoration. Prague has certainly changed with time but on the right day it is still capable of inducing a Bohemian rhapsody.

Beers to Czech Out

Beer is much more than just a mildly alcoholic beverage with which to celebrate the end of the working week for Czech Republicans, who consume 281 pints per person annually. The country produces some of the most highly-regarded beers in the world, such as Budweiser Budvar (no relation to the American beer) and Pilsner Urquell. But with brews from more than 100 breweries to sample, the Czech Republic's frequent beer festivals may provide the best opportunity to explore their products. Another perfect venue for beer drinking is the beer garden, especially in Prague when the sun is out. Settle down in Letna's beer garden, which overlooks the spires of the Old Town. For more serious research, head for the specialist beer shop Pivni Galerie where more than 200 varieties of bottled beer are sold. Indeed, the Czechs like beer so much that they'll even bathe in it. Try it yourself at the Chodovar Beer Spa in the cellars of the Chodvar brewery, a daytrip from Prague.

Dancing House

DENMARK

TIME DIFFERENCE GMT +1 (Central European Summer Time +2)

TELEPHONE CODE : +45

CURRENCY Krone

LANGUAGE Danish

NATIONAL TRANSPORT WEBSITE www.dsb.dk

POPULATION 5,400,000

SIZE OF COUNTRY 43,075 sq km (16,631 sq m)

CAPITAL Copenhagen

WHEN TO GO Summer in Denmark, from May to September, can be delightfully sunny and warm with long hours of daylight but this is when accommodation is at its most expensive. Unlike Sweden and Norway, Denmark has few winter sports: winters are dank and dark.

TOURIST INFORMATION www.visitdenmark.com

This small country, protruding into the North Sea from the north-western border of Germany, has a population of just over five million and is often considered the 'most satisfied' nation in the world. Whether this is due to Denmark's measured social policies, its very high standard of living or the sophisticated capital city, Copenhagen, isn't specified. Regardless, Copenhagen could never be called 'edgy', but if you have a taste for minimalist design, great food and excellent sightseeing it could be a rewarding alternative to other northern European cities such as Stockholm, Antwerp or Amsterdam.

COPENHAGEN

There's something about Denmark's capital. Whether it's the supremely well-adjusted people – Danes were judged the world's happiest nation in a survey by a British university – or the emphasis on slick design, few places are as relaxing and approachable as Copenhagen. This is city life on a small scale, with a carefully preserved medieval core, a quaint harbour and no high-rise buildings. As with many Baltic cities, in particular Stockholm, light and water play a large part in determining the city's moods. On winter days grey clouds can scud across the sky, and the dark evenings are perfect for sitting inside with a spiced winter beer called Yulebryg from one of Copenhagen's many microbreweries or exploring the Christmas market in the Tivoli Gardens. Two museums near Tivoli are worth a visit: Ny Carlsberg Glyptotek, at Dantes Plads 7, and the Nationalmuseet. Ny Carlsberg Glyptotek displays the rather eclectic personal collection of Carl Jacobsen ranging from Egyptian relics to French

A Day in Malmö

It might not rank alongside the Golden Gate or Millau bridges in terms of beauty, but the Oresund Bridge, which opened in 2000, allows motorists to drive from Copenhagen to Malmö in Sweden. The 16-km (10 mile) bridge, one of the world's longest, takes ten minutes to drive and at the end are the fabulous beaches and handsome city centre of Malmö.

HOW TO GET THERE
Scandinavian Airlines, British Airways, easyJet and BMI fly to Copenhagen from various UK airports. A much slower route is to take a ferry from Harwich to Esbjerg and finish the journey by train.

CONTACTS/FURTHER INFORMATION
www.visitcopenhagen.dk
www.natmus.dk
www.royalcopenhagen.com

The bustling Nyhavn area

Sunrise over Copenhagen

impressionism. The Nationalmuseet illustrates periods from Denmark's history, from the Vikings to the 20th century. It has particularly good exhibits for children.

In spring and summer, as daylight returns, you should get out and explore this charming capital. The medieval heart of the city can be covered on foot or bicycle – this will also allow you to wander down intriguing cobbled alleys and stop off at cafés. Much of Copenhagen is criss-crossed by canals and water taxis are a quick way of getting around. The Nyhavn canal, where Hans Christian Andersen lived, boasts a large number of restaurants in attractive period properties alongside the waterfront where you can enjoy the Danish specialities of pickled and smoked fish. Copenhagen's dining scene has hit a high in recent years with some well-received restaurants opening – but be aware that prices will compare with London and Paris.

Simple, functional and stylish: Danish design is world famous and the city's most famous son is perhaps the designer Arne Jacobsen. He created the world's first designer hotel, the Radisson SAS Royal Hotel, and numerous design classics, including the 'Egg' chair. Anyone with an interest in modern design will want to check out Copenhagen's best showrooms such as the Louis Poulsen showroom at 11 Nyhavn, specialising in lamps. The Royal Copenhagen department store at Amagertorv 6 showcases work by young designers. Christianshaven, just southeast of Nyhavn by boat, is also a good spot for galleries and design studios.

A Day at the Beach

Few people would consider Denmark for a beach holiday. The Mediterranean; yes. The Baltic; you must be joking. But summers in Scandinavia can be hot and sunny and the Baltic coastline of Denmark has some beautifully clean, sandy beaches. After all, this is the country that introduced the Blue Flag awards for clean, safe beaches. Many of the best beaches, such as Bornholm and Fyn, lie on islands but are easily accessible from Copenhagen. To reach Bornholm take a train to Ystad and a ferry from Ystad to Bornholm. The secluded beaches of Fyn, on the Jutland peninsula, are reached via the local capital, Odense, which was the birthplace of Hans Christian Andersen. There is a train service between Copenhagen and Odense.

ESTONIA

Estonia joined the EU in 2004 after decades as a Communist republic. The small, rural country hasn't looked back and, among former Soviet states, is a leading power in the technology industry. Its capital, Tallinn, benefits from the extra wealth but still has one of the most charming and beautiful old towns in the Baltics. Once labelled 'the next Prague', Tallinn has skilfully survived the stag party set as it has survived numerous invasions during its long and eventful history. Tallinn's medieval charm hides a modern, sophisticated and ambitious city.

TIME DIFFERENCE GMT +2 (Central European Summer Time +3)

TELEPHONE CODE +372

CURRENCY Kroon

LANGUAGE Estonian, Russian

NATIONAL TRANSPORT WEBSITE www.edel.ee

POPULATION 1,350,000

SIZE OF COUNTRY 45,200 sq km (17,452 sq m)

CAPITAL Tallinn

WHEN TO GO Winters in Estonia are harsh and dark. A snow and ice-covered Tallinn is attractive but most people prefer the spring (April to June) and autumn (September to October). Summers can be wet.

TOURIST INFORMATION www.visitestonia.com

014

TALLINN

HOW TO GET THERE
Estonian Air and easyJet fly to
Tallinn from London airports.
Tallinn's airport is very close to
the city.

**CONTACTS/FURTHER
INFORMATION**
www.tourism.tallinn.ee

*St Olaf's Church towers above
the Old Town.*

Don't be put off the Estonian capital by the reports of British stag parties laying waste to the city like rampaging Vandals. Any city that has been the subject of a tug of war between Sweden, Denmark and Germany and has survived 60 years of Soviet control can cope with a few drunken tourists. And the stag parties are right about something: Tallinn is perfect for letting your hair down.

The city is medieval beauty encapsulated, with a fascinating Slavic twist best seen in the classic onion-shaped domes of the Alexander Nevski Cathedral. The city centre's Old Town, Vanalinn, is a compact maze of cobbled alleyways often packed with sightseers during the summer months. The main thoroughfare is Pikk, a long street that runs from the Maritime Museum to the heart of the city, a rocky mound called Toompea where the Estonian Parliament building is located. Much of the revelry in Tallinn takes place in Raekoja plats (the Town Hall Square), midway along Pikk, but make sure you explore off the

beaten track and down side streets where many of the best bars can be found.

While tourists frequent Vanalinn, many of the locals socialise in the new city centre beyond Tammsaare Park. To reach sights that are further from Vanalinn you could join one of several guided bicycle tours of Tallinn. New openings in recent years include the KUMU art gallery in Kadriorg and the Museum of Occupation and Fight for Freedom, showing day-to-day life in Tallinn during the German and Soviet occupation from 1939 to 1991. Since the collapse of Soviet rule in 1991, Tallinn has boomed and is a model economy for other Baltic states. Tourism is far from the only source of income: IT is a rapidly growing industry, attracting expats, particularly from Scotland.

Eating in Estonia

Estonian cuisine is a marriage of simple, light Scandinavian flavours – such as pickled herring and beetroot – and hearty Eastern European dishes that stick to your bones in the country's cold winter. Think roasted and stuffed shoulder of veal or braised goose stuffed with apples and plums. In times gone by every inch of an animal's carcass had to be used: a particularly Estonian speciality is jellied meat (a terrine of a calf's head or sometimes pig's trotters) and blood sausages are also traditional. Carbohydrates are provided by potatoes and a black, sourdough rye bread, called *leib*. It's a rustic cuisine designed for economy and to fuel outdoor work. Meals are washed down with dark beers and mulled wines and are sometimes concluded with a glass of a Tallinn, Estonia's own liqueur. Approach with caution: it is available with an alcohol content of 50 per cent (100 proof), disguised by the sweet vanilla and cinnamon flavour.

Old Town backstreet

FINLAND

TIME DIFFERENCE GMT +2 (Central European Summer Time +3)

TELEPHONE CODE +358

CURRENCY Euro

LANGUAGE Finnish

NATIONAL TRANSPORT WEBSITE www.vr.fi

POPULATION 5,300,000

SIZE OF COUNTRY 338,145 sq km (130,559 sq m)

CAPITAL Helsinki

WHEN TO GO Finland is at its best in spring and summer. Helsinki has its share of snow in winter but it doesn't have the same Christmassy atmosphere that some other northern European cities enjoy.

TOURIST INFORMATION www.visitfinland.com

Helsinki, the Finnish capital, is an outpost of civilisation in a Scandinavian country that is predominantly covered by forests and lakes. Heading into Finland's backcountry – and there are plenty of tours that require either skis or hiking boots – is a significant undertaking, so most weekenders stick to spending their time exploring Helsinki's galleries and museums. One treat for anybody thrilled by architecture is the bold modernism on display in the city. And the art galleries are equally exciting.

HELSINKI

On the surface, Helsinki might seem like a quirky choice for a weekend break. Sunshine is often fleeting and there is no equivalent of the Colosseum or the Eiffel Tower. But Helsinki's appeal lies in its capacity to surprise and intrigue. On the cusp of Scandinavia and Slavic Europe, it's an unusual place but not so unusual as to provoke complete culture shock, although the language is utterly impenetrable.

Take Helsinki's restaurant scene. Several years ago the Finns were widely acknowledged to have a diet as bad as that of the Scots. Today, when you go into one of Helsinki's flashy new dining rooms you'll face a menu with dishes such as reindeer *carpaccio* (thinly sliced raw meat) and unfamiliar ingredients such as cloudberries.

A good starting point is a visit to the National Museum of Finland on Mannerheimintie, the broad thoroughfare through the city centre around which many of Helsinki's key sights are located, including the opera house and the parliament building. The museum covers Finnish history from prehistoric times to the present day. Helsinki's focal point is the Kauppatori, the market square on the south side of the centre where the fresh fish that plays such an important part in modern Finnish cuisine is landed. There's a fish market here that foodies will love where fresh snacks are served all day. To the west of the Kauppatori are two of the most up-and-coming neighbourhoods in Helsinki, the so-called Design District and Kamppi. These are where Helsinki's hippest hotels, such as Klaus K, and restaurants are opening. Shoppers should also make their way to these neighbourhoods for the best range of boutiques in the city. To see but not touch, Helsinki's Kunsthalle displays work in the applied arts by designers such as Arne Jacobsen and Eero Aarnio, inventor of the classic 'Bubble Chair', suspended from ceilings throughout the 1970s. It's undeniably quirky, but like Helsinki, makes perfect sense.

"Several years ago the **Finns** were widely acknowledged to have a **diet** as bad as that of the **Scots**."

HOW TO GET THERE
Finnair and British Airways fly direct to Helsinki from London Heathrow. You can also reach the city from Tallinn on the fast hydrofoil service between the two cities.

CONTACTS/FURTHER INFORMATION
www.hel.fi
www.taidehalli.fi

The Sparakoff Pub Tram

FRANCE

TIME DIFFERENCE GMT +1 (Central European Summer Time +2)

TELEPHONE CODE +33

CURRENCY Euro

LANGUAGE French

NATIONAL TRANSPORT WEBSITES
www.voyages-sncf.com; www.eurostar.com; www.ratp.fr

POPULATION 60,000,000

SIZE OF COUNTRY 543,965 sq km (210,026 sq m)

CAPITAL Paris

WHEN TO GO Paris, as the song suggests, is best in springtime but France is an all-year-round short break spot. Summer sees the beach resorts and roads of the Mediterranean fill up, while the alpine resorts are busy all year round: hikers and bikers in the summer and skiers and boarders in the winter. The west coast's Atlantic waves draw surfers in the autumn and many of the cities are at their most enjoyable outside the school holidays. France goes on general vacation during August.

TOURIST INFORMATION www.franceguide.com

Europe's number one holiday destination has had decades of experience welcoming travellers. France is a vast country and whatever the time of year there will be a corner of the country where you can spend a memorable weekend doing something you love; whether it's people-watching in Paris from a pavement café, sunbathing among the glitterati on the Côte d'Azur, surfing Atlantic rollers off Biarritz or just enjoying one of the country's 400 local cheeses in a sun-dappled village.

ANGERS

The Loire is France's longest river and it meanders from the Massif Central through some of France's finest wine-growing estates, from Sancerre to Saumur, on its way to the Atlantic. The medium-sized town of Angers (west of Tours) is your gateway into this French heartland. Angers is the capital of the Anjou, one of the most ancient counties of France, dating from the 9th century; during the Middle Ages it was even ruled by English kings.

The treasures of the Loire Valley – castles, châteaux, idyllic riverbanks – are easily accessible from Angers but, because public transport is limited, you will need to make your own way around. Angers itself also deserves at least a day of your time. The River Maine flows through the attractive town centre with the prize attraction, the *Tapestry of the Apocalypse*, sitting in the Château d'Angers on the right bank. The château, a fortress with 17 stone towers, was the home of the Duke of Anjou who commissioned the biblically-themed tapestry in 1375. It depicts the Battle of Armageddon, the Day of Judgement and other apocalyptic scenes from the Book of Revelation. It's one of the best, and most dramatic, examples of tapestry in France. Inspired by the tapestry, you could make your way up the river to the Cathédrale St Maurice, another early-medieval building. Cross the River Maine for the second of Angers's great tapestries, *Le Chant du Monde*, a 20th-century riposte to the Tapestry of the Apocalypse housed in the Musée Jean Lurçat in the La Doutre neighbourhood. It's no less gripping, depicting nuclear holocaust but also the wonder of life.

Take the end of the world off your mind by exploring the Loire's magical castles and châteaux. Two of the most beautiful, Chenonceau and Azay-le-Rideau are located to the east of Angers on the Loire in the Touraine region. This part of the Loire produces grapes that thrive on the chalky, flinty terroir, such as Chenin Blanc and Sauvignon.

HOW TO GET THERE
Flybe fly from Southampton to Angers.

CONTACTS/FURTHER INFORMATION
www.angersloiretourisme.com

Chenonceau Castle

017 AVIGNON

HOW TO GET THERE
Flybe fly from Exeter and
Southampton to Avignon.

**CONTACTS/FURTHER
INFORMATION**
www.avignon.fr
www.festival-avignon.com
www.choregies.asso.fr

Rue Joseph Vernet

In the south of the Rhône Valley, the fortified city of Avignon has stood guard over Provence for centuries. The site was prized by the Romans because it stood on a rocky outcrop but since the fall of the Roman Empire it has passed through the hands of numerous invaders. It is also surrounded by outstanding Roman sights, including Orange to the north and Arles to the south, where Vincent van Gogh painted some of

> "Avignon itself has enough historic **gems** to last a weekend of **sightseeing**."

his most memorable works in the 1880s, such as *Café Terrace at Night*. The key Roman ruins in Arles are protected by UNESCO World Heritage status and the city has a superb museum detailing its ancient history, the Musée de l'Arles et de la Provence.

Avignon itself has enough historic gems to last a weekend of sightseeing: the Pope was based in the city from 1306 to 1370 and its religious ties are highlighted by the spectacular Cathédrale Notre Dame des Doms, overlooking the Pont d'Avignon, the city's famous bridge. Avignon is noted for its annual festival, which takes over the city every July; accommodation will be hard to find at this time but outside of the summer months, Avignon makes an attractive and lively base for exploring western Provence.

No trip here would be complete without visits to Arles and Orange, where the open-air Roman theatre has such brilliant acoustics that a highly-regarded annual opera festival, the Chorégies d'Orange, has been held there since 1860. Head east into Provence's wilder interior and the mountains of the Luberon, where the highest peak in the area, the strangely barren moonscape of Mont Ventoux, looms over the fields of lavender. It was on the slopes of Ventoux that the British cyclist Tommy Simpson died competing in the Tour de France of 1967. A shrine marks the spot. South of Avignon lies the marshland of the Camargue, a natural park with its own breed of horses, managed by the Camarguais cowboys.

HOW TO GET THERE
Flybe fly to Bergerac from
Birmingham, Exeter,
Southampton, London
Gatwick, Manchester, Leeds-
Bradford and Edinburgh
airports.

**CONTACTS/FURTHER
INFORMATION**
www.bergerac-tourisme.com

Old Town, Bergerac

BERGERAC

Pleasant though Bergerac is, it earns its place here by being the doorway to the Dordogne, the south-western region of France long popular with holidaying British families. This part of France, to the east of Bordeaux, is defined by the River Dordogne, on which Bergerac lies. The river has carved a wide, steep-sided valley out of the limestone landscape and is the focal point for sunny days messing about in boats. Erosion has also played a part in other attractions of the area, such as the incredible Lascaux caves, east of Bergerac. This cave system, close to the village of Montignac, has walls covered in paintings dating from 15000 BC, depicting species of prehistoric animals and hunting scenes. Up to 2,000 individual paintings are spread throughout the cave system, including a 5-metre (17-foot) long painting of a bull in the Hall of the Bulls.

The Dordogne is better known to the local French as the *département* Périgord Pourpre, an area of bucolic pleasures. The small villages of the region produce some of France's most indulgent cuisine: foie gras, truffles and the liberal use of goose fat. You'll need to rent a car to make the most of the Dordogne as the best way of exploring is to take off into the countryside, stopping to eat at whichever village takes your fancy. Bergerac is on the western fringe of the Dordogne so follow the river upstream to reach areas like Périgord Noir (home of the cave paintings) and its beautiful but busy capital, Sarlat.

There's no need to venture into Bordeaux in the hunt for good wines either; Bergerac has some excellent vineyards of its own (look for Côtes de Bergerac) that can be better value than Bordeaux's big names. The town itself has an old core and modern suburbs, but don't expect to spend much time here when there is the rest of the Dordogne to discover.

HOW TO GET THERE
Ryanair fly from London
Stansted to Biarritz.

**CONTACTS/FURTHER
INFORMATION**
www.biarritz.fr
www.anglet-tourisme.com

St Jean de Luz

BIARRITZ

Just above the Spanish border, on the Atlantic coast, is one of France's original beach resorts. Biarritz's golden age was when European royalty, including Queen Victoria, holidayed in its grand palace (built for Napoleon's wife Eugenie) and sauntered along the seafront. The one-time whaling town swiftly became the chic playground of the rich and famous and is now returning to fashionability thanks to a mix of discreet celebrity fans for whom the Côte d'Azur is too tacky and an influx of well-to-do surfers searching for the perfect wave. Most surfers stay north of the town, while for a less glitzy experience, head south to the pretty harbour of St Jean de Luz. Biarritz itself has some excellent restaurants and stylish nightlife, and even a casino. But the real charms of the area, aside from the beaches, lie inland in the Pays Basque. This northern part of the Basque country, at the tail-end of the Pyrenees, has some excellent hiking (the GR10 path passes through St Jean de Pied Port) around villages decked out in thousands of red peppers hung out to dry.

Surfing

The southwest coast of France, part of the Aquitaine region, is the closest place to the UK with truly world-class waves breaking along 270 km (168 miles) of federally protected beaches, but it is the stretch from Seignosse south of Biarritz that interests surfers. Bruno Julia, who runs Hossegor-based Surf Trip (who offer surfing tuition) compares surfing one of Hossegor's bigger waves to climbing Everest. But there are plenty of more sheltered beaches with starter-sized waves. Biarritz apart, surf tourism is the mainstay of beachside towns, so everything is on hand. The breaks are beach rather than reef and they move about – seek local advice. Also ask the locals about the offshore currents, which can be very dangerous. Look for the clubs approved by the French Federation of Surf. Autumn brings the year's best surfing; base yourself behind one of the surfing beaches such as Hossegor or Anglet rather than in pricier Biarritz. Surf camps offer basic accommodation plus tuition packages.

BORDEAUX

The capital of Aquitane, Bordeaux, is a large, varied and handsome city, at least in the centre; the suburbs stretch for miles along the River Garonne. It's a city without any stand-out sights, where the most recognisable building is the twin-spired Cathédrale St. André, dating from the 12th century. A handful of museums are worth visiting, especially the Musée d'Aquitane one block from the cathedral and the small but rewarding Musée des Beaux-Arts behind the cathedral.

Bordeaux's old town lies on the west side of the Garonne and the Place St Pierre in Vieux Bordeaux is the hub of the city's fantastic restaurant scene. There's a large university in Bordeaux, creating correspondingly lively nightlife. But when you have finished partying in the city, there are few pleasures to beat settling down on a deserted, sandy Atlantic beach. The coastline from Bordeaux all the way down to Biarritz has hundreds of quiet beaches, backed by pine forests. Head in the opposite direction, inland, and you'll encounter Bordeaux's main claim to fame: the world's most famous vineyards.

Wine

The great estates of the Bordeaux regions are some of the most venerable and expensive names in wine: Lafite-Rothschild, Margaux, La Tour Haut-Brion and Mouton Rothschild. A bottle of vintage claret (the name used to describe red wines from Bordeaux collectively) from any of these producers can set you back a small fortune. Best known for producing reds, each particular regional appellation in Bordeaux, such as Pomerol on the 'Right Bank' (east of the Gironde river) and Médoc on the 'Left Bank' (west of the Gironde), has its own character, determined by the year's climate, the soil and several other factors. About 500 million bottles of wine are produced in the Bordeaux area, although the quality is variable. And where there are vineyards, there are châteaux, some of the most graceful old mansions in France. Even if you're not a vinophile, a wine-tasting tour of just a few châteaux is a wonderful way of spending a weekend in Bordeaux.

HOW TO GET THERE
easyJet fly to Bordeaux from Bristol and Luton.

CONTACTS/FURTHER INFORMATION
www.bordeaux-tourisme.com
www.vins-bordeaux.fr

Place de la Bourse, Bordeaux

021

BREST

HOW TO GET THERE
Flybe fly to Brest from Exeter, Southampton, Birmingham and Manchester.

CONTACTS/FURTHER INFORMATION
www.brest-metropole-tourisme.fr

Mont-St-Michel

Brittany's charms lie in bracing walks in the fresh air of this idiosyncratic corner of France, and its distinctive Breton culture. Adjoining Normandy, Brittany has a rugged coastline that, despite a climate similar to the south of England, still attracts thousands of holidaymakers every year; between those rocky headlands are soft, sandy beaches and rocky inlets that children love exploring.

Brest itself, at the tip of the Brittany headland, is best left as soon as possible. It was a major naval base and consequently devastated during the Second World War. But south of Brest, beyond the Crozon Peninsula, is some of Brittany's least frequented coastline, around the Pointe du Raz and the île de Sein. Continue south to Carnac to see Europe's most impressive pre-historic site: hundreds of standing stones (called menhirs) placed north of the village. Brittany's numerous Neolithic sites are extremely important archaeologically and offer intriguing glimpses of the ancient ties with Cornwall and other Celtic areas. Bretons are fiercely proud of their culture and heritage and have preserved many of their traditions in the form of poetry and music. The Inter-Celtic Festival in Lorient every August is the world's leading showcase of Celtic culture, attracting performers and visitors from Scotland, Wales and Ireland as well as Spain and France.

Mont-St-Michel

Lying on the border with Normandy, Mont-St-Michel was originally an island between the two *départements*. Its place in French history – outside of Paris, it is perhaps France's most iconic building – began in AD 708 when a tiny chapel was built on a rock by the Bishop of Avranches. Over the years the chapel became a church then an abbey and a fort. It was a prison during the French Revolution and finally returned to being a monastery in 1969. It is now one of France's most popular tourist attractions so arrive early to beat the crowds. A new footbridge from the mainland means that visitors no longer need to have a tide timetable when making the crossing.

HOW TO GET THERE
Ryanair fly to Carcassonne from Liverpool, East Midlands and London Stansted airports.

CONTACTS/FURTHER INFORMATION
www.carcassonne.org

Carcassonne

CARCASSONNE

Deep in the Languedoc-Roussillon region of southern France, Carcassonne is a strikingly beautiful fortress city, its turreted castle walls visible for miles around. Carcassonne is one of Europe's best-preserved medieval forts thanks to the efforts of French conservationists and UNESCO, but it does mean that the city is invaded by masses of sightseers during the holiday season; come outside of July and August for a less congested view of this fantastic place.

The best time to see Carcassonne is at twilight, when the souvenir shops have closed and the massive, golden stone walls are floodlit and the open-air cafés and restaurants of the old town are filled with chattering diners. The old town is split into two parts: the Cité (the citadel) and the Ville Basse (the low town). The Cité is the heart of Carcassonne, an ancient fortress with narrow, twisting streets designed to slow invaders. It all looks as if the resident Cathars have only just been chased out, rather than 800 years ago – in fact the suspiciously pristine appearance is due to a controversial restoration beginning in 1844. No matter, Carcassonne is still a joy to explore. Start with the lovely church of St Nazaire; climb the tower for fabulous views over the city. The walls surrounding the Cité can also be walked, although you will have to join a guided tour.

Cassoulet

It's hard to pin down the exact origin of this dish, with Toulouse, Castelnaudary and Carcassonne claiming ownership. What is certain, however, is that the bean, pork and duck fat stew is a symbol of France – and a rural, defiant France at that. The dish is supposed to have been concocted during the siege of Castelnaudary, 36 km (22 miles) west of Carcassonne, in the Hundred Years War when the townspeople pooled all the remaining food they had and cooked it together for a last meal. Thus fortified, they routed the besieging English army; although that part may be apocryphal. There are also plenty of conflicting recipes for the traditional *cassoulet*. A few ingredients are beyond debate: white beans, pork (not necessarily Toulouse sausage) and stock (typically using duck fat, pork bones and trotters). It's a mainstay of menus in Languedoc-Roussillon, so you can compare *cassoulets*.

023 DEAUVILLE

HOW TO GET THERE

Several cross-channel ferries operate services to ports in Normandy. The closest port is Le Havre, served by LD Lines from Portsmouth. Brittany Ferries sail between Portsmouth and Caen, to the south of Deauville. Trains for Normany from Paris depart the Gare St-Lazare.

CONTACTS/FURTHER INFORMATION

www.deauville.org

Deauville promenade

While Cannes grabs the headlines and the paparazzi's flashbulbs, the north of France has a highly-regarded film festival of its own, at Deauville in Normandy. Deauville's film festival, the American Film Festival, takes place in September and is noted for the low-key attitude of its fans and stars; here there are few red ropes dividing some of cinema's biggest names from their fans. The promenade's beach huts bear the names of Hollywood legends who have attended the festival.

Deauville, in the Calvados county of Normandy, was a favoured summer retreat for fashionable Parisians, so much so that Coco Chanel launched her career in fashion here in 1916. Trends are cyclical and so Deauville is returning to its heyday; it's a glamorous resort with something of an old-world feel thanks to a cabaret, casino and summer jazz festival. But like many northern beach resorts, it's at its best when the sun is shining; try not to visit out of season.

Calvados is packed with other attractions, not least the eponymous apple brandy. To the north of Deauville, Honfleur is an enchanting port that has caught the eye of many painters: local artist Eugène Boudin is thought to have started the impressionism movement with his attempts to catch the gentle hues of Honfleur's port and the Norman sky. Claude Monet himself, the master of impressionism, lived in Giverny in the neighbouring Eure region, a short drive down the A13 from Honfleur.

Calvados has several outstanding châteaux that make interesting afternoon daytrips from Deauville, including Château de Fontaine-Henry, Château St Germain-de-Livet and Château de Vendeuvre. But for many visitors, the most compelling reason to visit Normandy is to view the sites of the D-Day landings that helped end the Second World War. Much of the Norman coastline was involved, from Arromanches-les-Bains, where a museum and cinema explain what went on, to Caen, site of the Mémorial de Caen, a museum dedicated to peace.

"The promenade's beach huts bear the names of Hollywood legends who have attended the festival."

HOW TO GET THERE
easyJet fly to Grenoble from
Bristol, Bournemouth,
Birmingham, Luton and
London Gatwick. Ryanair fly to
Grenoble from Glasgow,
Liverpool, East Midlands and
London Stansted airports.

**CONTACTS/FURTHER
INFORMATION**
www.grenoble-isere.info

Méribel ski resort

GRENOBLE

In the winter, the airport queue for flights to Grenoble will be spiky with skis. The city is the main point of entry for the Dauphine region of the French Alps, where many of France's best-known ski resorts are established, most no more than an hour or two from Grenoble by car. There's an enormous array of terrain available from beginners' slopes to some of the steepest, most severe runs in Europe. Resorts in the vicinity of Grenoble include Serre Chevalier, La Plagne, Val Thorens, Les Arcs, Méribel, Alpe d'Huez and perhaps the most successful all-round mega-resort, Les Deux Alpes.

French ski towns are not generally noted for the beauty of their architecture. Most of the modern buildings are functional rather than quaint, and Grenoble is no exception. But its breathtaking location, at the confluence of the Drac and Isère rivers and with a backdrop of snow-capped mountains is a welcome compensation. In a past life it was a major industrial centre and it is still an important research hub for the nuclear industry. There's a large university in the city, keeping the nightlife lively throughout the year. The summer season in the Alps is just as busy as the winter, with mountain bikers flying down the same mountainsides the skiers use in the winter.

La Grave

If Les Deux Alpes is where youngsters can strap on their first pair of skis and form their first snowplough, La Grave might be where the very best of them end up, skiing some of the scariest terrain in the world. Where the massive Les Deux Alpes resort is groomed and slickly organised, La Grave is little more than a tiny mountain village with just one cable car and no ski patrols. But with 1,829 m (6,000 ft) of off-piste descent, through vertiginous, rocky couloirs, La Grave has become a place of pilgrimage for extreme skiers. These expert skiers may need ice-climbing or rappelling skills to reach the start of the most technical runs. There's just one local mantra in this wilderness: 'Don't fall'.

025

HOW TO GET THERE
easyJet fly to La Rochelle from Bristol and London Gatwick, Ryanair from London Stansted and Flybe from Southampton, Birmingham and Manchester.

CONTACTS/FURTHER INFORMATION
www.larochelle-tourisme.com

La Rochelle harbour

LA ROCHELLE

North of Bordeaux lie some of the most unspoiled beaches in France. These broad swathes of sand are edged with pine trees and sand dunes. In August there is barely space to move, even on the largest beaches such as Royan, but at other times of the summer they are a delightful haven. The prettiest town in the area is La Rochelle; arguably the most handsome of all French seaside resorts. A programme of careful conservation has ensured that this port has retained all its character, while concessions to the annual tourist influx, such as a pedestrianised centre, add to the relaxing air of the resort. The main thoroughfare, the rue du Palais running from the old port to the place de Verdun is the star of the town, lined with 18th-century buildings. Seafood restaurants are another major strength of this family-friendly town.

Inland, the River Charente flows lazily past reedy river banks and fishermen. Life is lived at a leisurely pace in the Poitou-Charente region and on the Île de Ré, off La Rochelle.

Île de Ré

A road bridge connects the Île de Ré with the mainland but the island is definitely a world of its own. It has been described as the Hamptons of France, a rarefied holiday spot for the Parisian elite who might consider the South of France a little too *arriviste*. With more than 100 km (62 miles) of cycle paths around the 30 x 5-km (19 x 8-mile) island and plenty of bike rental shops, you don't need to bring a car onto the Île de Ré; it's the sort of place where Parisian holidaymakers wearing clam-digger trousers and an elegant jersey pedal from beach to café. Many of the best beaches are on the south side of the Île de Ré while the capital, St Martin-de-Ré, is on the north shore. The harbour town grew prosperous through trade and has stalwart fortifications to repel invading, often British, navies.

LIMOGES

Driving from the neighbouring Périgord to the Auvergne could almost be classed as time travel: where the Dordogne bustles with holidaymakers, the Auvergne is a vast and sleepy region with a primeval, volcanic landscape. The largest city in this central *département* of France is Limoges, a no-frills sort of place that is best known for producing some of France's best porcelain. Limoges is the capital of the Limousin, a fertile farmland that tourism has largely bypassed. Some of the cheapest property prices in France are here, although that is changing gradually. The principal attraction of the area is the Parc des Volcans d'Auvergne, east of Limoges. The volcanoes – Puy de Dôme is the most famous – form part of the Massif Central, a vast expanse of rugged hills, gorges and forests. Many of France's largest rivers have their source in the Massif Central, including the Loire. But the area is also the source for many brands of mineral water: Volvic is a small town close to the largest city in the Auvergne,

Clermont-Ferrand. And just north of Clermont-Ferrand is Vichy, one of France's leading spa towns where wrinkled bathers wallow in sulphurous hot springs and drink the supposedly curative waters.

The most accessible volcanoes are those of the Monts-Domes, oddly rounded, grassy craters with some little-used single lane roads winding through them. The Monts-Dore volcanic region is much more mountainous, containing the Massif Central's highest point, the Puy de Sancy. Hikers roam the hills in summer but should be aware that the Massif Central doesn't have the infrastructure or the safety resources of the Alps or Pyrenees. Plan your routes carefully.

The third volcanic region of the Auvergne is the Monts du Cantal to the south of the Parc. The three peaks of the Monts, the Plomb du Cantal, Puy Mary and Puy de Peyre-Arse, form a single volcano's cone, one of the largest in the world. There are some demanding walks in the area but most people come just to take a picture.

HOW TO GET THERE
Flybe serve Limoges from Southampton, Manchester and Newcastle.

CONTACTS/FURTHER INFORMATION
www.tourismelimoges.com

St. Michel d'Aiquilhe above Le Puy

027

LYON

HOW TO GET THERE
easyJet fly to Lyon from
London Stansted.

**CONTACTS/FURTHER
INFORMATION**
www.lyon-france.com
www.nicolaslebec.com
www.bocuse.fr
www.opera-lyon.com

France's second city matches its capital for art, culture and, above all, gastronomy, with the advantage of being a lot closer to the Alps and the Côte d'Azur. Lyon is a business-like place but there are plenty of diversions to help wile away the time between restaurant sittings.

Lyon's centre, the Presqu'ile, lies on the wedge of land between the rivers Rhône and Saone, both of which flow through the city. This is where you'll find the Opera House, a 300-year-old landmark now modernised with a glass roof and an auditorium lined with black wood and gold. Lyon's opera season is highly regarded but there are also excellent ballet productions in the city. Art lovers will also relish the Musée des Beaux Artes housed in a former abbey in the centre of Lyon. Seventy rooms display the second largest art collection in France, featuring pieces from all over the world. Don't miss the newly added collection of impressionist paintings or the French art from the 19th and 20th centuries, which is also a strong point.

North of the Presqu'ile, the working district of La Croix-Rousse was once the heart of Lyon's silk trade, which relied on the rivers. Today this is a

good place to shop and eat among the 'traboules' or secret alleyways. In the first *arrondissement*, on the west bank of the Saone, Vieux-Lyon is dominated by the Basilique Notre-Dame de Fourviere, an overblown church offering good views of the city. Then, when you've walked off some calories, it's time to get back to what Lyon does best: gastronomy.

Gastro Lyon

Many of the most highly-rated restaurants in France can be found in Lyon. Combining the flavours of the north and south of the country, Lyon has become a place where chefs make a name for themselves. Two of the biggest names are Paul Bocuse, chef-patron at L'Auberge du Pont de Collonges just north of Lyon, and up-and-coming star Nicolas le Bec, chef at his eponymous eateries in Lyon. Bocuse also has five bistros in the city but a more down-to-earth option is to eat at one of Lyon's *bouchons*, a traditional restaurant serving local specialities.

Statues on the Opera House

HOW TO GET THERE
Ryanair fly to Montpellier from London Stansted.

CONTACTS/FURTHER INFORMATION
www.ot-montpellier.fr

The Millau Viaduct

MONTPELLIER

There's no single, stand-out reason to visit Montpellier, but most people who spend time in the capital of Languedoc-Roussillon leave promising to return. Montpellier is a modern yet historic university town to the east of the Langudoc with a very youthful population and a booming business sector, making it a fun and dynamic city in which to spend a night or two. The focal point for much of the city's cultural life is the place de la Comédie, also known as l'Oeuf (the egg). The square's Comédie Opera House is one of the most highly-rated venues in the country, attracting high-calibre performers. The 19th-century opera house has a modern counterpart, the Berlioz Opera House, which opened in 1990 and is one of the largest opera houses in France. L'Oeuf is also a good place for bar and café hopping, although the city's 60,000 students also congregate in place Jean-Jaurés. During the day there are several interesting sights to tick off. As a university city, there are also plenty of quirky museums, including the Musée d'Anatomie. Saturday sees a huge flea market appear under the Pont du Gard aqueduct.

The Millau Viaduct

A drive up the A75 towards Millau – taking an hour and a half in favourable traffic – will lead you over one of the world's modern engineering marvels: the Millau Viaduct. This beautiful 2.5-km (1½-mile) suspension bridge over the Tarn valley was designed by Sir Norman Foster and opened in December 2004. The breathtakingly elegant road-bridge soars 250 m (820 ft) above the valley floor, curving from north to south, and on misty mornings it can look like you're driving above the clouds. The seven delicate, 343-m (1,125 ft) high pylons hardly look strong enough to support the world's highest road-bridge; the deck alone weighs 36,000 tonnes. The project cost 400 million euros; some of which will be offset by the toll to cross the bridge. It has become an attraction in its own right, a contemporary Eiffel Tower.

029

NICE

HOW TO GET THERE
easyJet fly to Nice from seven UK airports. Flybe fly to Nice from Exeter and Southampton.

CONTACTS/FURTHER INFORMATION
www.nicetourisme.com
www.visitmonaco.com
www.ot-saint-tropez.com

Nice is the capital of the Côte d'Azur and the main entry point for the thousands of sun seekers and *bon viveurs* who arrive every year on this fabled coast. Yet this large city is regarded as second best by many; too gritty for the millionaires, too bustling and busy for holidaymakers. But Nice has always had an excellent selection of museums and galleries, 19 at the last count, plus plenty of the old town's Italianate architecture survives. Even on sunny days, when being indoors isn't an option, there's the beachfront Promenade des Anglais to stroll along and interesting views of the city to take in from Le Château Park.

The narrow streets of Vieux Nice (Old Nice) have a pleasant mix of trendy boutiques and bars, complemented by new nightclubs. There are chapels and churches galore, although the most eye-catching church is the Russian Orthodox Cathedral to the west of the city. The city's stand-out museums include the Musée d'Art Moderne et d'Art Contemporain, with a world-class collection of pop and modern art. Henri Matisse wintered in Nice and the Musée Matisse gives a great overview of his life and work with paintings from all periods of his life.

For many people, Nice is all about grazing on light, Provençale meals and relaxing at the pebbled beach; like many beaches along the Côte d'Azur, Nice's is for posing rather than serious sunbathing or water sports.

East of Nice

To the east of Nice lie a couple of the favourite haunts of footballers and racing car drivers: Monaco and Monte Carlo. Monaco is a surreal place; it is an independent principality, ruled by the Grimaldi family, where property prices have long lost touch with reality thanks to its tax-free status. This tiny strip of land, totalling just 485 of the most densely populated acres in the world, plays host to some of the world's richest people, many of whom gamble at the casinos of Monte Carlo, one of Monaco's four quarters. Monte Carlo remains as glamorous as ever and the city's belle époque casino still attracts high-rolling gamblers and socialites; dress accordingly if you want to get in.

An altogether more down-to-earth experience is on offer at Menton, just shy of the Italian border to the east of Monaco. Arguably, this is the most enjoyable resort of the Côte d'Azur influenced by Italy and with a pretty beach and promenade. Closer to Nice, another pleasant spot on the coast is Beaulieu. From here you can walk to Cap Ferrat where many of the most expensive villas in the south of France are located, many owned by celebrities.

West of Nice

West of Nice, the cities of St Tropez and Cannes thrive on the celebrity circuit. Cannes is the hard-edged, noisy end of the French Riviera; to get the most out of it you have to be the type of visitor who enjoys the buzz of a city with busy roads and cramped hotels. The city's calendar revolves around the annual film festival in May, when every room will be booked; similarly, July and August are difficult times to visit. An out-of-season trip, however, should let you enjoy the beach and museums a bit more. An interesting daytrip from Cannes is to the town of Grasse, a short drive inland. This is where many of the major perfume brands design their fragrances, using the Provençale flowers and other ingredients. Between Cannes and Nice lies Antibes, one of the most exclusive corners of the Côte d'Azur. Many artists lived on the Côte d'Azur for the quality of the light, including Pablo Picasso. The Musée Picasso in the Château Grimaldi in Antibes exhibits some of his work from this period. When the super-rich want to keep a low-profile they stay in Antibes; when they want to be seen, they go west to St Tropez, a playground for bronzed socialites ever since Brigitte Bardot first frolicked on its beach. The best spot for people-watching – the main pastime in St Tropez – is to grab a table at a café in the old town.

Negresco Hotel

030

PARIS

HOW TO GET THERE
Eurostar from London's St Pancras International station is the preferable option from the British capital. easyJet fly to Paris Charles de Gaulle from Bristol, Belfast, Liverpool, Luton, Glasgow, Edinburgh and Newcastle. Flybe fly to Paris Charles de Gaulle from several UK airports including Norwich, Belfast and Edinburgh.

CONTACTS/FURTHER INFORMATION
www.parisinfo.com
www.musee-orsay.fr
www.louvre.fr
www.quaibranly.fr

Ever-quicker transport links from the rest of Europe, and London in particular, make 'this timeless town' more of a weekend winner than ever before. It would take a lifetime of weekends to uncover every secret of this remarkable city, the most-visited capital in Europe, so the best advice is to plan ahead and don't bite off more than you can chew. Paris benefits from a cheap and efficient public transport system, including, as of 2007, fleets of rental bicycles, and it is relatively compact. However, the very best sights do demand at least half a day of your attention.

Highlights must include the Musée d'Orsay, in the 7th *arrondissement*, with its renowned impressionists collection and the Renaissance works in the Musée du Louvre. The Louvre, in particular, is one place to savour in small and frequent bites. The Musée du Quai Branly opened in 2006 and contains examples of indigenous art and ethnographic items. Don't miss the 'living wall' by architect Jean Nouvel. A surprise choice for favourite Parisian sight might be the Musée Rodin in the 7th *arrondissement*, where you can see *The Kiss* indoors and meet *The Thinker* outside.

Some critics argue that Parisian restaurants are resting on their laurels. It's certainly true that cafés in highly visited areas are not renowned for their warmth of welcome but this is also a city of superlative dining; just look at the number of Michelin-starred restaurants in the 8th and 16th *arrondissements* alone. After dinner, Paris doesn't match London, Berlin or Barcelona for bars and clubs. Instead, enjoy the city from a new perspective. Sights such as the Notre Dame cathedral – even more Gothic in the darkness – are floodlit. Paris's bridges and boulevards look even more beautiful at night and the slower pace of life suits the romantic wanderer.

Alternative Paris
Tours of Parisian cemeteries are a popular option. They've evolved over the centuries to become atmospheric, miniature cities. And, like cities, many have their own celebrity citizens. Père Lachaise cemetery boasts the most famous grave in Paris, that of Doors' singer Jim Morrison. Literature lovers may prefer Montmartre cemetery near Sacré Coeur church where the writers Stendhal, Emile Zola and Alexandre Dumas are buried. The cemeteries are noted for their sculptures, which range from the poignant to the bizarre.

However, there's one place in Paris that takes the bizarre to a whole new plane. Deyrolle is a renowned taxidermist's on rue du Bac, near the Musée d'Orsay: but it's rather more like a museum of stuffed animals, including deceased zoo animals such as buffalo and zebra posed in surreal tableaux, than a shop. Weird and wonderful.

"Paris's bridges and boulevards look even more beautiful at night and the slower pace of life suits the romantic wanderer."

Sacré-Coeur Basilica

031

HOW TO GET THERE
Ryanair fly from London
Stansted to Pau.

**CONTACTS/FURTHER
INFORMATION**
www.pau.fr (in French only)
www.pyreneesguide.com
www.bearn-
basquecountry.com
www.lourdes-infotourisme.com

Palais Beaumont

PAU

In the foothills of the Pyrenees-Atlantiques, Pau is an excellent base for exploring the fascinating Pays-Basque and Bearn regions at the western end of this mountain range. The Pyrenees differ from the Alps in several substantial ways and are much less developed. Unlike the Alps, which have many major ski resorts, skiing in the Pyrenees is a low-key activity. Andorra to the east, for example, is known as much for its duty-free shopping as its ski slopes.

But the section of the Pyrenees around Pau is the most interesting of the whole range. The Pays-Basque includes three historic Basque provinces on the French side of the border with Spain: La Soule, Labourd and Basse-Navare. Here are some of the least tamed mountains in the south of France, such as the valleys of the Aspe and Ossau where some of the best hiking can be found. You can stay in mountain refuges or in some of the excellent Logis de France in the small towns and villages of the Bearn. Outdoor types can hike, paraglide, bike, climb and kayak in stunning scenery.

Lourdes

Southeast of Pau is one of the busiest towns in France. Lourdes was an undistinguished Pyrenean village when in 1858 a 14-year-old girl, Bernadette Soubirous, began having visions of the Virgin Mary in the Grotte de Massabielle. This was taken as a sign that something celestial was afoot and the town has gradually grown to become a major site of pilgrimage for Catholics. Today, 150 years after Bernadette's first vision, the streets are lined with shops and stalls selling every conceivable souvenir, the more kitsch the better, as well as empty containers in which to store the holy water of Lourdes. There are also 230 hotels in the town, the highest concentration in France. The shops and hotels are outnumbered only by the constant tide of sick people who queue in the hope of being cured in the town's cave.

PERPIGNAN

This rugby-loving city is at the eastern tail of the Pyrenees, where they slope into the Mediterranean. It's a handy gateway to an overlooked corner of the Mediterranean where the sea meets the mountains, although you probably won't want to stay in Perpignan itself; it's pleasant enough, with a definite Spanish feel, but not as idyllic as many of the outlying towns and villages such as Prades.

Inland, the landscape is dominated by the Pic du Canigou, the highest mountain at this end of the Pyrenees. Fortunately, you can drive most of the way up on a narrow, rutted track that is steep in places (you might want to hire a four-wheel-drive car for this). The walk to the summit takes you through woodland and up rocky, ravined slopes, and the views from the top, on a clear day, are uplifting. Canigou plays an important part in Catalan mythology – like the Basques at the opposite end of the Pyrenees, regional culture extends across the Spanish border.

If you do stay in nearby Prades, there are several excellent sights in the area, including the abbey of St Michel-de-Cuxa, one of the finest in the country. South of Perpignan, the village of Céret boasts an excellent museum of modern art: Georges Braque and Pablo Picasso painted together in Céret in 1911.

As you make your may towards the coast, the land becomes flatter and incredibly fertile, with fields of fruit trees surrounding small farmsteads. The highlight of the coastline here is the fortified port of Collioure, a wonderful place to explore for a day, with a pebbly beach and a historic palace and harbour area. The town was a favourite of many artists, including Picasso and Henri Matisse, who was inspired by the blue skies of Collioure. North of Perpignan, food-lovers should stop at Narbonne's superb daily market in the Halles de Narbonne to pick up some local specialities.

"Georges **Braque** and Pablo **Picasso** painted together in Céret in 1911."

HOW TO GET THERE
Ryanair fly from London Stansted to Perpignan. Flybe fly from Southampton to Perpignan.

CONTACTS/FURTHER INFORMATION
www.pyreneesguide.com
www.perpignantourisme.com
www.ot-ceret.fr

Pic du Canigou

GERMANY

TIME DIFFERENCE GMT +1 (Central European Summer Time +2)

TELEPHONE CODE: +49

CURRENCY Euro

LANGUAGE German

NATIONAL TRANSPORT WEBSITE www.bahn.de

POPULATION 82,500,000

SIZE OF COUNTRY 357,868 sq km (138,174 sq m)

CAPITAL Berlin

WHEN TO GO German cities – especially Berlin – are exciting all year round. For winter sports, Munich is the best choice, while sightseers should wait until May for the best weather. Late summer (September) is often the best time to visit Leipzig or Cologne, when the crowds have departed and you have the cities to yourself. There are festivals throughout the year.

TOURIST INFORMATION www.germany-tourism.co.uk

Perhaps the most underrated weekend destination in Europe, Germany delivers nights out in some of Europe's hippest clubs, world-class sightseeing and a history that is never less than enthralling. Cologne, Munich and Stuttgart are some of Europe's most dynamic cities while the German capital, now undivided, is certainly one of the most exciting places you'll visit, with nightlife to rival London and a defiantly independent culture. Most German cities pride themselves on their green spaces and it's also easy to escape the urban environment to explore Germany's great forests and rivers.

HOW TO GET THERE
Berlin has two airports, Tegel
and Schoenefeld. British
Airways flies to Tegel and
easyJet flies to Schoenefeld.
Other airlines serving Berlin
include Ryanair, Air Berlin
and Germanwings.

**CONTACTS/FURTHER
INFORMATION**
www.berlintourism.de
www.juedisches-museum-
berlin.de

Modern sculpture abounds

BERLIN

Berlin is a city of surprises. Whether you're climbing the inside of the Norman Foster-designed glass dome on the Reichstag, encountering all-nude sunbathing in the city centre's Tiergarten park or dancing all night at a warehouse-style club in what was once Soviet-allied East Germany, Berlin has a way of confounding expectations. It is arguably the most exciting, creative and liberal city in Europe at the moment; as if freedom from the responsibility of being Germany's economic powerhouse (Munich and Frankfurt are the corporate and financial centres of Germany) has allowed the capital to pursue the art of having a good time.

Historically, Berlin has expertise in this area. In the 1920s and 1930s, as befits the birthplace of Marlene Dietrich, Berlin was famous for its cabaret scene. Dietrich herself became a Hollywood star after playing a femme fatale in *Der Blaue Engel* (The Blue Angel), released in 1930. These days, Berlin cabaret is returning to the heady years of the 1920s, made famous by Liza Minelli in *Cabaret*. Large venues such as the Wintergarten

are packed with tourists but there is also smaller, more niche cabaret that is well worth seeking out. In other areas, Berlin has shrugged off nostalgia. Almost two decades after it's fall the Berlin Wall it has virtually disappeared from the city landscape. In the years following the fall of the wall, East Berlin suffered economic hardship and only now have businesses and services flooded back into deprived neighbourhoods, like air into a vacuum. The East also has some of the cheapest property prices in Germany, which makes it attractive to artists.

Berlin has several well-defined neighbourhoods and to make the most of its attractions and nightlife you'll have to plan your weekend carefully; it is a very large city. The central district of Mitte is the equivalent of London's West End; it's the bustling heart of the city, with the grand boulevard Unter den Linden as the main artery. Unter den Linden stretches from the Brandenburg Gate (where the city's top hotels, such as the Adlon are located) to Schlossplatz. Just beyond the Brandenburg Gate, the Reichstag has been the

Brandenburg Gate

seat of Germany's Bundestag since 1999 when the British architect Norman Foster completed the glass dome covering the building's bombed-out shell. Both these sights should be at the top of your must-see list. Mitte's Auguststrasse is the focus of Berlin's art scene with a large number of galleries. For boutique shops, explore the streets of Mitte or Prenzlauerberg to the northeast. Continue west from Unter den Linden and you'll enter the Tiergarten, one of the world's largest city centre parks. In the opposite direction, Friedrichshain is a youthful, hipper and increasingly gentrified neighbourhood – this is where young Berliners hang out in funky bars and cafés while monitoring their laptops and Blackberrys. Berlin has long had a strong alternative culture, which has influenced the entire fabric of the city. But as Berlin has grown, the anti-corporate counter-culture has been gradually pushed out of the city centre and into the gritty but funky neighbourhood of Kreuzberg; this is a cosmopolitan area where you will find organic health food shops rather than McDonalds. Berlin's large Turkish community run markets, bakeries and steamy hammams here but the best reason to visit Kreuzberg is the Judisches

Museum, an astonishing, provocative and eloquent museum designed by Daniel Libeskind. The zigzagging, zinc-clad building is intended to not only portray what happened to Berlin's Jewish population but also involve all your other senses to suggest disorientation, fear and distrust – it's a remarkable project.

Nightlife in Berlin

Berlin's nightlife is second to none. It is the place to discover your previously dormant taste for cabaret or Wagner. However, the city's party reputation is largely based on its nightclubs where the soundtrack is typically unrelenting techno and house. Clubs come and go – previously influential names such as Tresor are long gone – and the annual Love Parade, a springtime rave that rolled through the city, will decamp for the next few years to cities in the Ruhr region. The hottest club in 2007 was Berghain, a weekly rave in a disused power station in Kreuzberg where anything goes at the marathon 36-hour parties.

COLOGNE

Germany's number one tourist attraction isn't in hip Berlin or high-flying Munich. It's in Cologne, and it's the Dom. Cologne's cathedral, blackened after years of life in Germany's industrial heartland, is a mesmerising building with the most imposing pair of towers in the ecclesiastical world. Work began on the cathedral in 1248 and it took, amazingly, until 1880 to finish – you can understand why it took so long. The cathedral's bell, nicknamed 'Fat Peter', is the world's largest free-swinging church bell and inside there's a shrine said to contain the bones of the three Magi. Lit up at night, it stands over the River Rhine like a beacon from the heavens. It's a staggering building, but just one of 250 churches in Cologne. The Dom is in the heart of a pedestrianised zone on the west bank of the Rhine that is crammed with outstanding museums and galleries. On summer days the open-air riverside restaurants are packed with people. Next to the cathedral, the Romisch-Germanisches Museum is built over the site of a Roman villa and contains artefacts from the Roman period up to early medieval Cologne. Highlights include an important collection of Roman glass and items from the wealthiest

Roman households. Moving onward, the collection of modern art in the Museum Ludwig is a primary-coloured antidote to the Roman relics. Peter and Irene Ludwig were ardent collectors of modern art, acquiring work by Roy Lichtenstein, Andy Warhol and Pablo Picasso.

Cologne is Germany's oldest city and perhaps its most cosmopolitan, having been occupied by Romans, French and Prussians. Make a sortie of your own to this fantastic German city.

Carnival in Cologne

Think Carnival and you probably think of Rio de Janeiro or Venice. Perhaps even Notting Hill, but not Cologne. However, Cologne's German population celebrates Carnival with a good-humoured enthusiasm – up to three million people attend the parades and the vast majority are in some sort of costume. The five days of Carnival start on the Thursday before Shrove Tuesday with the biggest parades taking place on Sunday and Monday. The German love of beer does nothing to dampen proceedings.

HOW TO GET THERE
BMI, easyJet and Germanwings fly to Cologne from UK cities. New high-speed trains also connect Brussels, Paris and Amsterdam with Cologne.

CONTACTS/FURTHER INFORMATION
www.koeln.de
www.museum-ludwig.de

Banks of the Rhine, Cologne

035 FRANKFURT

HOW TO GET THERE
Lufthansa flies to Frankfurt from several UK airports.

CONTACTS/FURTHER INFORMATION
www.frankfurt-tourismus.de
www.deutsches-filmmusuem.de
www.staedelmuseum.de

Christmas Market in Romer Square

Frankfurt is a small city with big city ambitions. It is Germany's financial centre and boasts the most futuristic skyline in Germany and Europe's tallest building, but it remains an approachable and interesting place with some of the best museums and galleries outside Berlin. The south side of the River Main, which bisects the city, has some of the most intriguing neighbourhoods, such as the Römerberg with medieval quarters reconstructed after the Second World War and now punctuated with small private art galleries. There are many other museums, such as the German Film Museum and the excellent Städel Museum.

Sealing the city's cultural reputation, Frankfurt was the birthplace of Johann Wolfgang von Goethe (in 1749) and his house is now a fascinating step back in time to the 18th century. Frankfurt's world-class Old Opera House might also look that old but it was actually rebuilt in its neo-classical style after the war and is a superb venue for visiting performers. A good night out Frankfurt-style typically begins in a bar or restaurant in the Sachsenhausen district on the south bank of the Main and ends in the nightclubs of Hanauer Landstrasse to the east.

Castle Tour

Bavarian castles are elegant, ethereal confections that seem to have come straight from the pages of a fairytale. So, it's not for nothing that a road trip, starting in Würzburg and finishing in Füssen is called the Romantic Road. It's an extremely popular route with up to two million people per year taking their time and visiting some of the castles along the way. Whether you choose to drive or cycle the 349-km (217-mile) route the closest airport is Frankfurt International and accommodation in the towns and villages along the Romantic Road range from quaint B&Bs to old-fashioned hotels. Don't miss King Ludwig II's most eccentric castle, the Neuschwanstein Castle, high on a rocky promontory. Supposedly, it was the inspiration for Sleeping Beauty's castle in Disney's film. Sadly, King Ludwig was declared insane before his castle was completed: it's indeed a fine line between genius and madness.

HOW TO GET THERE
Flybe flies to Hamburg from Birmingham while British Airways and Lufthansa fly there from London Heathrow. Flights from other UK airports are offered by easyJet, Ryanair, Air Berlin and Germanwings.

CONTACTS/FURTHER INFORMATION
www.hamburg-tourism.de

Isebekkanal in Eppendorf, Hamburg

HAMBURG

Germany's second-largest city can puzzle the first-time visitor. As with many port cities, its seedy red light district is a long-standing part of the cityscape – Hamburg's Reeperbahn (the district's main street or 'sinful mile') being more famous than most – but the city also has a high concentration of green spaces and is one of the wealthiest in Europe. For example, the botanical gardens, Planten un Blomen, are right in the heart of the city, offering respite without charge.

Situated on the River Elbe, which empties into the North Sea at the toe of Denmark, Hamburg has long been crucial for Germany's import and export trade. Its massive harbour, one of the world's largest and a UNESCO World Heritage site, has been redeveloped to bring stylish eateries to a once purely industrial part of the city. In the same way that the city's fortunes rest on its proximity to water, so too has its layout been governed by the Elbe. Although the city has been rebuilt twice, after fire and war, Hamburg has more bridges than Venice. The best way to see the city is from the water (there are water taxis and sightseeing boats) or by walking along the waterfronts – the key sites are located between the Alster, a lake, and the Elbe.

Located just off the An de Alster waterfront walk, the Kunsthalle is the city's main gallery, filled with important works by German artists.

The Beatles Connection

Hamburg played an important role in the formative years of the Beatles. In the early 1960s, the first incarnation of the Beatles, featuring Stuart Sutcliffe, played at several Hamburg clubs, such as the Indra and the Star Club in the vicinity of the Reeperbahn. Various members of the band were deported back to Britain – at 17 years of age, George Harrison was breaching child labour laws while Paul McCartney and Pete Best were accused of arson – but the band returned to the German city in early 1961, where they recorded their first professional tracks.

HOW TO GET THERE
Air Berlin flies direct to Leipzig Halle airport from London, Manchester, Belfast and Glasgow. Berlin Schoenfeld airport has a direct rail link to Leipzig taking two hours, making it a convenient alternative. Flights to Leipzig-Altenburg airport require a long transfer.

CONTACTS/FURTHER INFORMATION
www.leipzig.de

City Hall Dome

LEIPZIG

Way over to the east of Germany, Leipzig is a very different proposition to the west German cities of Frankfurt, Stuttgart and Cologne. Unlike those cities, Leipzig was part of the German Democratic Republic although the Communist habit of erecting grey concrete wastelands didn't afflict Leipzig to any significant extent – just turn a blind eye to the occasional 1960s tower block. The Saxon city is noted for its compact but beautiful city centre, which is extensively pedestrianised. Architecture ranges from typical stone-built Saxon buildings with steeply-canted roofs to an array of exciting modern constructions such as the decidedly insectoid Central Stadium erected for the 2006 football World Cup. And how many cities can boast a BMW factory designed by Pritzker-prize winning female architect Zaha Hadid? Don't miss the Old City Hall, built in 1557 and probably the city's most notable building.

As well as being an architectural field trip, Leipzig was East Germany's most cultured city. It was the home of Johann Sebastian Bach for the last 25 years of his life, until his death in 1750. The composer, now a venerated figure in Leipzig, was appointed the choir master of the Thomaskirche, an elegant Lutheran church where his remains are buried. Opposite the church a museum fills in the rest of Bach's life.

Forget conventional sightseeing. Leipzig has two fascinating exhibitions, both dealing with the post-war period of Communist rule in the city. This was a time of fear, paranoia and, eventually, freedom. The first site is the Zeitgeschichtliches Forum at Grimmaische Strasse 6. Then make your way to the site of the former headquarters of the Stasi, the GDR's secret police, at Dittrichring 24. This museum displays some of the brutal and bizarre tactics that the Stasi used against their fellow Germans.

But Leipzig is much more than a trip back in time. It has some excellent shopping arcades, especially during the Christmas market, and in its restaurants you'll find that the specialities of Saxony are lighter than bratwurst and sauerkraut.

MUNICH

This is Germany's self-assured, money-making powerhouse. Other Germans like to categorise Munich as a city of 'laptops and lederhosen', where espresso-fuelled yuppies are forever rushing from one meeting to another with no time to appreciate what a beautiful city they live in.

And Munich is certainly geographically blessed. It is within striking distance of superb alpine skiing and in the summer the mountains and lakes are perfect playgrounds for mountain bikers and water sports enthusiasts. As the German novelist Thomas Mann noted, 'Munich sparkles'.

It is an ambitious, fast-moving place; like London or San Francisco it attracts plenty of outsiders seeking work in the city's media, IT and car industries (Munich is the home of BMW). Even with a population drawn from all over the world, Munich has a very strong Bavarian identity, based largely on excessive consumption of bratwurst and beer. The marriage of hops, barley and water is celebrated annually at the Oktoberfest, which is certainly the world's largest drinking session and probably its largest festival too.

With affluence comes responsibility and Munich has certainly invested in its galleries and museums, such as the excellent Pinakothek arts complex which houses everything from Old Masters to contemporary photography in a series of buildings to the southwest of the city.

The Oktoberfest

The world's biggest beer festival is not something to take on lightly. The best accommodation gets booked up months in advance and the scale of it beggars belief: about seven million people sink beers during the two-week event. The first Oktoberfest was held in 1810 and it was decided that October had the best weather for beer drinking: not too hot and not too cold. During its first centenary in 1910, 120,000 litres of beer were drunk. By 2006, seven million litres were consumed, as well as hundreds of thousands of sausages and portions of fried chicken. 1,600 waitresses are employed in 14 tents and 1,000 tonnes of rubbish is generated. And don't even think about the loos.

HOW TO GET THERE
BMI, Lufthansa, British Airways and easyJet all serve Munich from various UK airports.

CONTACTS/FURTHER INFORMATION
www.muenchen-tourist.de
www.pinakothek.de
www.oktoberfest.de

Oktoberfest

039 STUTTGART

HOW TO GET THERE

Germanwings flies to Stuttgart from London Stansted. The high-speed train from Paris takes less than four hours.

CONTACTS/FURTHER INFORMATION

www.stuttgart-tourist.de
www.museum-mercedes-benz.com
www.porsche.com

You don't have to be a committed petrol head to enjoy Stuttgart – but it might help. The south-western German city is arguably the birthplace of the automobile; it's certainly the base for some of the finest names in motoring, from Maybach to Mercedes-Benz. The city was also where the Volkswagen Beetle was conceived. But don't imagine that this is a post-industrial, gridlocked hell. Far from it: Stuttgart is a green, leafy city with a pleasant historic centre and a penchant for beer. There are plenty of diversions for when the thrum of exhaust pipes begins to pall: a planetarium, botanical gardens and the startlingly Cubist Kunstmuseum where the 5,000 piece art collection was started by an Italian count.

"The city was also where the Volkswagen **Beetle** was **conceived**."

Germany's Motor City

Art comes in many forms. For some it is a piece of music, for others a painting. But for a select group of obsessives, there's nothing more beautiful than a motorcar. Not just any car, of course, but a classic. And, for some reason, Germany seems to have produced more of these aesthetic marvels than any other nation. Between them, Porsche and Mercedes have created classics – such as the Mercedes 300SL with its distinctive gullwing doors and the iconic Porsche 911 – and Stuttgart is where their fans come to pay their respects. The city houses the headquarters of both Porsche and Mercedes-Benz and both companies have must-see museums containing some of the fastest and most desirable cars in the world. Porsche's museum, in Porscheplatz to the north of the city, has a small selection of historic racing cars on show at any one time. But the main attraction is Mercedes-Benz's new 150-million euro museum which opened in 2006. The museum covers more than a century of motoring, from Daimler's first Merc in 1902 to some of the sleekest cars ever designed. There are 160 cars exhibited in this nine-story temple to the internal combustion engine and they all have a story to tell.

Inside the futuristic Mercedes-Benz Museum

GREECE

This country of 1,400 islands has been the perfect summer holiday destination for generations. The Cyclades, Sporades and Ionian islands might be sandy, summery paradises but the Greek capital is best experienced out of the peak season, when its unparalleled ancient ruins – the Parthenon and the Temple of Zeus – are less crowded and hot. Although the Olympics of 2004 brought some improvements to the city's public transport, the streets still resemble a melée. Come for the history and don't expect to relax.

TIME DIFFERENCE GMT +2 (Central European Summer Time +3)

TELEPHONE CODE +30

CURRENCY Euro

LANGUAGE Greek

NATIONAL TRANSPORT WEBSITE www.ferries.gr

POPULATION 11,000,000

SIZE OF COUNTRY 131,957 sq km (50,949 sq m)

CAPITAL Athens

WHEN TO GO Rural Greece closes down for the winter months, while Athens is considered a more habitable place out of the searing summer heat and stifling pollution.

TOURIST INFORMATION www.gnto.gr

ATHENS

HOW TO GET THERE
British Airways and easyJet
have regular flights from
London airports. easyJet also
flies to Athens from Berlin,
Paris and Milan.

**CONTACTS/FURTHER
INFORMATION**
www.gnto.gr

The Teseion

While the Greek capital is typically a stopover for travellers heading for the Greek islands, if you follow some basic advice it can be a fascinating place to spend a weekend. The most important tip is not to visit during the oppressively hot summer months, when many of the city's restaurants and shops will be closed and the pollution will be at its worst. However, since the city hosted the 2004 Olympics several new projects – an extended metro and tram system to the coast – have helped improve the quality of life in the city. It's not just public transport: there are new attractions too. At the base of the Acropolis, a new museum designed by Bernard Tschumi will house some of Greece's most important antiquities in state-of-the-art galleries. There will even be a magnificent, naturally-lit gallery for the Parthenon marbles, 88 of which were removed from the Parthenon by the Earl of Elgin in 1806. This museum, 30 years in the planning, has been delayed year after year but it is scheduled to open in 2008.

The history of Athens begins 3,000 years ago. It was one of the cradles of European civilisation, where philosophers such as Plato, Aristotle and Socrates sought to make sense of the world around them in the 5th century BC. Few European cities can rival Athens for historic sights: at the Acropolis and the Parthenon you can tread in the footsteps of ancient Athenians and at Areopagus Hill you can stand where St Paul preached. Recent pedestrianisation of the streets that surround the Agora and the Acropolis have helped make the Plaka district much more appealing too. Nightlife is also resurgent in Athens; the swanky suburb of Glyfada is where many waterfront bars and clubs can be found. Note that you might find the city is surprisingly expensive; three millennia of history doesn't come cheap.

HUNGARY

Once the heart of the Ottoman Empire, Hungary is gradually returning to its historic role as a bridge between Western and Eastern Europe. Always one of the more economically and socially liberal of the former Communist states, Hungary has blossomed in recent years. But its capital, Budapest, remains an intoxicating, bohemian city with a vibrant musical culture and as many bridges as Prague. Indeed, if you liked Prague, Budapest is the next step. Although surrounded by mountains, Hungary's landscape is flat and laced with rivers.

TIME DIFFERENCE GMT +1 (Central European Summer Time +2)

TELEPHONE CODE +36

CURRENCY Forint

LANGUAGE Hungarian

NATIONAL TRANSPORT WEBSITE www.mav.hu

POPULATION 10,000,000

SIZE OF COUNTRY 93,030 sq km (35,919 sq m)

CAPITAL Budapest

WHEN TO GO Spring and autumn are magical times to visit Hungary, if a little wet. As a largely flat country, winter sports are limited to just keeping warm. Summers can be baking hot and in August many businesses, even in Budapest, close for the month. May, June, September and October are the best months to visit, weather-wise.

TOURIST INFORMATION www.hungary.com

041

BUDAPEST

HOW TO GET THERE
easyJet, Jet2 and Wizzair fly to
Budapest from UK airports.

**CONTACTS/FURTHER
INFORMATION**
www.tourinform.hu
www.gellertbath.com

Divided by the River Danube, the two halves of the Hungarian capital, Buda and Pest, revel in the nickname the 'Paris of the East'. Less exposed than Prague and larger than Tallinn or Riga, Budapest is one of the hottest post-Communist destinations in Europe. It has sights (and bridges) to rival the Czech capital, an ashamedly hedonistic side and enough *fin-de-siècle* glamour for anyone. Music-lovers in particular will relish Budapest, where musical traditions run from the Hungarian composers Béla Bartók and Franz Liszt, who taught in the city for several years, to the choreographed chaos of Magyar gypsy bands. Live music is easily found in Budapest, especially during the summer when free rock concerts take place in some of the city parks and nightclubs let their DJs play outside. Winter is a time to stay indoors and listen to classical recitals in the city's art nouveau concert halls.

Before the Soviet occupation, Budapest's salons and cafés were a flamboyant fixture on the Grand Tour of Europe. The city had an art-loving reputation and even after the Soviet regime took control, Budapest was a haven for *émigrés* and artists. But foreign money is transforming the city faster than ever. Stylish and expensive hotels are springing up; leader of the pack is the Gresham Palace Hotel (owned by the Four Seasons Group), which maintains a link with the past through its outstanding art-deco café.

Restaurants in Budapest are undergoing a similar transformation. The national cuisine was always rich and tasty – think goulash and roast goose – but new restaurants are introducing modern menus to beautiful old venues. The dining scene is particularly strong around the city square Liszt Ferenc tér while the grand Andrassy Boulevard – the Champs-Elysées of Budapest – remains the street of choice for big-budget hotels and restaurants. The wine available in restaurants is also improving rapidly, with expertise from France and Argentina transforming Hungarian vineyards. All in all, it's an exciting time for food and wine lovers to visit.

However, you should definitely also make time for some traditional sightseeing while in Budapest.

The sprawling city (get a travel card or be prepared to take a lot of taxis) has some stunning sights: the Gothic House of Parliament, based on London's, the palace complex on the top of Castle Hill, which includes the Hungarian National Gallery, and the Museum of Fine Arts between Andrassy and City Park. Many figures from Budapest's past, Lenin and Marx among others, are reunited in the quirky Szobor (Statue) Park; you'll need to take a taxi here.

Shoppers won't have to travel too far: Kiraly Street has an interesting selection of boutiques. Blessed with great food, a thriving music scene and an attractive city centre, Budapest is going places.

Budapest's Spas

If your idea of a perfect weekend involves being doused in warm water and pummelled and stretched to within an inch of your life, Budapest won't disappoint. The city ranks as one of the best in the world for spas thanks to 118 naturally occurring hot thermal springs that gush 70 million litres of water daily. Make a date at the Gellert Spa by Liberty Bridge, perhaps the city's top spa and certainly its most photographed thanks to the marble columns and mosaics in the steam rooms and pools. The hot springs are rich in minerals that can help skin and joint conditions and robust masseurs take the no-pain-no-gain approach – this is a traditional Hungarian spa rather than a watered-down boutique version. You can spend up to a whole day at the Gellert, although the sister hotel is on its last legs. Don't expect scented candles or ambient music: Hungarian spas are cheap, rambunctious places where locals catch up with gossip and play a game of chess. Other good spas to try are the Ottoman Kiraly Baths, which date from the 16th century, and the neo-baroque Szechenyi Baths in the City Park where the 15 unisex pools are popular with locals.

Statue in front of parliament

ICELAND

TIME DIFFERENCE GMT +0

TELEPHONE CODE +354

CURRENCY Krona

LANGUAGE Icelandic

NATIONAL TRANSPORT WEBSITE www.bsi.is

POPULATION 300,000

SIZE OF COUNTRY 102,820 sq km (39,699 sq m)

CAPITAL Reykjavik

WHEN TO GO Whatever the time of year, this is
an enthralling country to visit. During the winter
Reykjavik is shrouded in darkness and the
months between November and February are
when you're most likely to see the Northern
Lights. Iceland begins freezing over around
October or November and doesn't thaw until April
or May. Then comes Icelandic summer, which is
short but bright and energetic.

TOURIST INFORMATION www.visiticeland.com

At a fresh-faced 20 million years old, Iceland is the youngest country
in Europe, floating above the Mid-Atlantic ridge where the European
and North American tectonic plates join. Just a three-hour flight from
London Heathrow and three hours from Boston, it's an island where
Europeans and Americans meet to explore a surreal landscape of
barren lava fields and sulphurous geysers. Despite the harsh
surroundings, Iceland's capital, Reykjavik, is an enormously appealing
and approachable city – although 'large village' might be a more
appropriate description. And there's nightlife here as hot as any
sizzling volcano.

REYKJAVIK

With a population of just 300,000, two-thirds of which live in the capital Reykjavik, Iceland's influence reaches far beyond what its size would suggest. Although the city is shrouded in darkness and snow for much of the year, it is one of the most striking cities in the world, an otherworldly place heated by subterranean geothermal energy and populated by charismatic and largely blonde citizens.

Architecturally, Reykjavik is an unsettling mix of traditional, low-level buildings designed to withstand winter weather and some modernist constructions such as the love-it-or-hate-it Hallgrimskirkja church, the beautiful, minimalist interior of which is even more astounding than the concrete shell. Another Reykjavik landmark is the revolving restaurant at the top of the Perlan, a round ball of a building that provides the city's hot water. Architecture aside, the key reasons to visit Reykjavik are the capital's social scene –

concentrated in just a couple of streets, such as Laugavegur, in the city centre – and the island's lunar landscape complete with fuming volcanoes and raging waterfalls, accessible even if you're

The Blue Lagoon

A short bus ride from central Reykjavik, the Blue Lagoon is one of Iceland's unmissable attractions. It doesn't sound enticing: a series of communal pools beside a power station, surrounded by a sulphurous odour. But the bathtub-hot pools are incredibly popular with young and old, local and visitor alike. The pools are filled with hot seawater that is rich in minerals and unusually buoyant; you can float in relaxed bliss even as snow falls. The pools are not deep so non-swimmers need not worry and you can hire towels at the visitor centre.

HOW TO GET THERE
Icelandair fly to Reykjavik from London Heathrow, Manchester and Glasgow.

CONTACTS/FURTHER INFORMATION
www.visitreykjavik.is

Thermal Swimming Pool, Langardalur

here for just two or three days. The outdoor life is deeply ingrained in the Icelandic population and you can try snowmobiling on glaciers or riding on hardy little Icelandic ponies.

In recent years Reykjavik has acquired an entirely justified reputation for glacial coolness with a night scene as hot as the famous thermal springs. What's more, Icelandic people are friendly, even whimsical: after all, this is a country where a majority of the population claims to believe in trolls, elves and *huldufolk* (hidden people).

Glacial lake

Off-roading

GPS, laptop, satellite phone, winch, snow jack and shovel: it's not wise to cut any corners on a road trip in Iceland, where the landscape is so inhospitable that American astronauts trained here for the moon landings. The national highway, Iceland's only paved road, is a ring road running all the way around the perimeter of the island. It's 1,328 km (825 miles) long, so it's not much use if you're in a hurry to get from one side of the island to the other. The alternative is driving across a landscape that has produced one-third of the world's lava flow in the last 400 years. And land that isn't jagged black rock is probably under one of Iceland's 20 glaciers, which cover 11 percent of the island. River crossings are fraught with danger, mountain roads are closed until the end of June and the glaciers' crevasses can swallow vehicles whole, should you be unfortunate enough to drive into one. It's not surprising that a country as unique and extreme as Iceland has spawned a vehicle as unique and extreme as the superjeep. These 4x4s on steroids are fitted with 112-cm (44-inch), balloon-tired wheels and super-powerful 300bhp engines. In the back there's often a bed and the jeep can heat water for days at a time – not that there's much need for it in a country that has more than 250 hot springs. Several Reykjavik-based outfits, such as Iceland Excursion, let visitors get a taste of off-roading Iceland-style. You'll get the chance to drive up and down Wolf Mountain, which overlooks Reykjavik, before tackling some of the island's many river crossings and off-road playgrounds of the Torfaera (hell fire) club, a specifically Icelandic sport in which drivers in customised, 800bhp buggies power as far up a near-vertical slope of black volcanic dust as they can before either roaring over the summit or rolling down backwards. Rules about driving on sensitive surfaces are strictly observed, as are safety regulations.

REPUBLIC OF IRELAND

The 'Celtic Tiger': that's how Ireland's buoyant economy has been described. Despite the popular perception of a fun-loving, good-humoured nation, Ireland is deadly serious about moving onward and upward. Fortunately, that ambition also extends to giving its visitors an even better time. Dublin has long been a fixture on the weekend break circuit and there's always the option to spend time exploring Ireland's smaller, less-visited towns and cities too. Often they are gateways to stunning natural scenery as well as usually boasting a strong local cuisine and culture.

TIME DIFFERENCE GMT +0 (Irish Summer Time +1)

TELEPHONE CODE +353

CURRENCY Euro

NATIONAL TRANSPORT WEBSITE www.irishrail.ie

POPULATION 4,300,000

SIZE OF COUNTRY 70,282 sq km (27,136 sq m)

CAPITAL Dublin

WHEN TO GO Ireland's lush, green countryside is the result of a high rainfall all year round, as weather fronts sweep in off the Atlantic. Summer – July and August – is when you're least likely to need an umbrella but the main attractions are at their busiest. St Patrick's Day (17 March) is another time when accommodation will be in short supply.

TOURIST INFORMATION www.irishrail.ie

043

CORK

HOW TO GET THERE
Aer Lingus and Ryanair have frequent services to Cork's small airport.

CONTACTS/FURTHER INFORMATION
www.discoverireland.ie

St Colman's Cathedral

Think of Cork as a Dublin in miniature, without the stag and hen parties and the faux-Oirish sentiment. This magical city is one of Ireland's most southerly outposts – Corkonians prefer to call it the real capital of Ireland – and a great base for exploring the fertile counties of Kerry and Cork. It offers a much more restful city break than Dublin although the Guinness still flows freely in the pubs should you wish to carouse all night – although if you really want to impress the locals order a Beamish, the local stout of choice. The first impression of Cork is a watery one: the city is one of the world's largest natural harbours and fresh fish catches are still landed and sold in the English Market. The harbour front is a postcard-worthy assortment of colourful townhouses and open-air cafés, which also line the sides of the River Lee, the braided waterway that runs through the heart of Cork. It is this al fresco attitude to life and the city's many canals that give Cork its continental flavour.

Eating out in Cork also lives up to this engaging setting. As with many harbour cities, Cork's food and drink scene is much better than average so it's an exciting destination for enterprising foodies. One of Ireland's leading cookery schools, Ballymaloe, is just 32 kilometres (20 miles) east of Cork and the English Market on Princes Street, which began business in 1610, is one of Europe's finest food markets. Locally produced bread, cheese, meat and seafood harvested from the Atlantic are just waiting to be discovered. While, in nearby Kinsale, the restaurant capital of Ireland, those ingredients are employed in some of the best dishes you're likely to find in Ireland.

As befits a previous European Capital of Culture (in 2005), Cork has plenty to excite culturally-inclined visitors, such as the new, timber-clad Lewis Glucksman Gallery on the University College campus. But sightseeing in Cork is really all about working up an appetite for the next meal.

> "It is the **al fresco** attitude to life and the city's many canals that give Cork its continental **flavour**."

HOW TO GET THERE
Ryanair, Aer Lingus and British Airways have frequent services to Dublin from various UK airports.

CONTACTS/FURTHER INFORMATION
www.visitdublin.com

The Temple Bar, Temple Bar

DUBLIN

The Irish capital has long been a popular weekend destination. It doesn't have the historic marvels of Rome or the sights of Paris – instead it offers more than 1,000 drinking dens serving deliciously chilled Guinness and a rich vein of repartee. In recent years, however, Dublin has moved upmarket and is now one of the trendiest locations in Ireland. It's much harder to find a cheap meal but the choice of eateries has expanded, with a restaurant for every taste. The city, and Ireland's new-found upward mobility has attracted celebrity investors too, with pop stars such as Huey from the Fun Lovin' Criminals and Bono from U2 buying into bars and hotels. The glitz has rubbed off, with Bono's Clarence Hotel being one of the most fashionable places to rest your head and Huey's Dice Bar in Queen Street becoming the venue of choice for a gritty but friendly night out. For keen drinkers, other alternatives to the tourist-traps of Temple Bar include the Central Hotel Library bar, an atmospheric book-lined venue above the Central Hotel's lobby, the Stag's Head, a large, lively pub, and Anseo, a funky, down-to-earth bar in the Village Quarter.

St Patrick's Day

Bloomsday isn't the only major celebration in Dublin. St Patrick's Day, the annual celebration of one of Ireland's patron saints on 17 March, has taken over the world, with green-hued festivals in cities from New York to Sydney. It's not the largest (that is probably in New York) but Dublin's St Patrick's Day parade is the centrepiece of a five-day festival that involves the consumption of large quantities of Guinness.

The River Liffey by night

Dublin is divided by the River Liffey and although there is not much of a class divide between north and south Dublin, the north of the city remains less gentrified than the south. One of the south's key attractions is the Guinness Storehouse. The famous bitter black drink is no longer fermented here, but the visitor centre and tour are Ireland's most popular attractions. Unsurprisingly, the tour finishes with a pint of Guinness. Not all attractions are alcoholic: the National Gallery of Ireland has a free-to-view collection of Irish and European artworks. Most visitors will want to combine a bit of both: beer and culture. And there's no better way of doing that than following in the footsteps of Dublin's many writers.

Literary Dublin

Few European cities have inspired as many writers as Dublin and, over the years, the city has reciprocated the compliment, providing many Irish and foreign writers with a roof over their heads and myriad pubs for when writer's block strikes. Some of the greatest names to have been born or lived in Dublin are the 17th-century satirist Jonathan Swift, Bram Stoker, the author of *Dracula* and the playwrights and wits Oscar Wilde and George Bernard Shaw. Later, William Butler Yeats would become Dublin's most famous poet, while the 20th century saw Samuel Beckett and Flann O'Brien achieve critical acclaim. Many of these writers studied at Dublin's Trinity College, where lectures open to the public are held in the Oscar Wilde Centre and dramas are staged at the Samuel Beckett Theatre. From April to October visitors can be guided around the college by current students. You can also learn more about Dublin's literary tradition at the Writers Museum in Parnell Square. But one writer above all has made the Dublin landscape his own: James Joyce, who was born at 41 Brighton Square in 1882. Joyce's *Ulysses*, published in 1922, was set during the passage of a single day in Dublin (16 June 1904) and that day now sees an annual re-enactment of scenes from the novel in landmarks across the city. Known as Bloomsday after the book's hero, Leopold Bloom, 16 June is an opportunity for Joyce fans to dress up in Edwardian costume and indulge in such seemingly random acts as ordering a gorgonzola cheese sandwich and a glass of Burgundy in Davy Byrne's pub or join a guided walking tour that might better be described as a pub crawl across Dublin.

GALWAY

The delights of the wild west coast of Ireland can be accessed from Galway. Ireland's third largest city is just at the heel of Connemara, one of the most remote and romantic regions of Ireland. The city also overlooks the Aran Islands, once described by poet Seamus Heaney as the 'three stepping stones out of Europe.' More recently the trio of Aran's islands have competed to host an annual festival founded on the television comedy show *Father Ted*. Although it is no stranger to the modern world, this is a side of Ireland that hasn't been influenced by the Celtic Tiger effect; things are done here much as they always have been and there are no Starbucks selling lattes. Instead, this part of Ireland has managed to keep some secrets of its own, such as some of the very best fly-fishing streams in Europe. And along the crenellated west of Ireland there are some world-class surfing and sea-kayaking spots – weather permitting.

Galway itself is an up-and-coming city with a strong musical tradition. If Dublin is for drinkers and Cork for foodies, then Galway is for music-lovers – although you'll find a hearty meal and a pint of Guinness just as easy to come by here too. The annual Galway Arts Festival in July, the highlight of the cultural calendar, is rivalled only by Galway's annual International Oyster Festival in September, a riot of shucked shells and seafood. The best way to appreciate Galway is to browse the waterfront and criss-cross the bridges over the River Corrib, keeping an ear out for live Celtic music sessions at pubs such as the Tig Coili.

The Ring of Kerry

Some way south of Galway, on Ireland's meandering roads, the Ring of Kerry is a famous looping road trip around the bucolic green fields and wind-lashed shores of County Kerry. However, the route is plagued by tour buses and sightseers in cars. An alternative is to take an eight-day cycling tour of Kerry's back roads, exploring the quiet lanes of Ivereagh and the Dingle peninsula with Cycling Safaris.

HOW TO GET THERE
Aer Arann flies to Galway from several British cities. Ryanair flies to Shannon airport, 89 kilometres (55 miles) south of Galway.

CONTACTS/FURTHER INFORMATION
www.irelandwest.ie
www.cyclingsafaris.com

Spiddal Beach

ITALY

TIME DIFFERENCE GMT +1 (Central European Summer Time +2)

TELEPHONE CODE +39

CURRENCY Euro

LANGUAGE Italian

NATIONAL TRANSPORT WEBSITE www.ferroviedellostato.it

POPULATION 59,000,000

SIZE OF COUNTRY 301,245 sq km (116,311 sq m)

CAPITAL Rome

WHEN TO GO Avoid Rome, Venice and Florence in the height of summer, when the heat and congestion make even these beautiful cities feel like hard work. Instead visit them during spring and autumn. The foot of Italy also suffers from extreme heat in the summer.

TOURIST INFORMATION www.italiantourism.com

Delectable food and wine, noisy red sports cars and a faultless eye for style: just a few of the things the Italians do well. Italy, like France, can offer something for everybody, but romance is a commodity you can find almost anywhere in Italy. From the crumbling buildings and Renaissance artworks of Florence to Tuscan vineyards or exuberant Neapolitan restaurants – Italy can excite passion effortlessly. There will be no shortage of 'only in Italy' moments. For outdoor sports, the north of the country is one of Europe's prime spots for alpinism while the south has its own fascinating mythology. This is a country where one weekend is never enough.

HOW TO GET THERE
British Airways and Ryanair fly
to Bologna from UK airports.

**CONTACTS/FURTHER
INFORMATION**
www.bolognaturismo.info
www.emiliaromagnaturismo.it

Neptune Fountain

BOLOGNA

Bologna, the capital of the Emilia-Romagna region, is an unbeatable weekend destination for sightseers who want to combine culture with superb food. If you're going to indulge yourself, there are few better places in Italy than the city known as La Grassa ('the fat one'). Great ingredients are at the heart of Emilia-Romagna – the region is responsible for prosciutto ham and Parmegiano Reggiano cheese from Parma and balsamic vinegar from Modena – and Bologna's restaurants and shops ensure its status as the gastro-capital of Italy.

This is a distinctively northern city, with solid buildings and hearty cuisine to keep the winter chill out. Pasta dishes in Bologna betray a French influence, often using butter instead of olive oil – stuffed tortellini and lasagnes are hardly summer food so consider visiting Bologna out of the peak season, especially if you can catch one of the world's best classical music festivals, the biannual Bologna Festival.

Bologna is renowned as a city passionate about culture and intellectual pursuits. After all, this is where the University of Bologna appointed Umberto Eco, author of *The Name of the Rose* and many other books, Professor of Semiotics. The university quarter, to the east of the historic city centre, and its 100,000 students dominate life in Bologna and have attracted high-tech firms to the city, adding to its affluence (luxury car manufacturers Maserati and Lamborghini are also based in the vicinity). Student nightlife is centred on Via Zamboni and good, affordable food is readily available from the city's basic osterias.

To work off all the calories, explore the city's relaxed and uncrowded medieval heart. The brick-red architecture isn't as delicate as that of Rome, Florence or Venice but it is still an engrossing place to explore. Many of the city's 42 museums are located around the Piazza Maggiore and Piazza del Nettuno, in between the grand palaces and churches. There are also 40 kilometres (25 miles) of covered arcades of shops to explore, including some of the best food shops in the world.

HOW TO GET THERE
Ryanair flies to Brindisi from
London Stansted.

**CONTACTS/FURTHER
INFORMATION**
www.pugliaturismo.it

Brindisi church

BRINDISI

Brindisi itself is an unremarkable port but it is the gateway to Italy's most unsung region, Puglia. Puglia is the heel of Italy, covering the southeast tip of the country. Loved by Italians, it receives relatively few foreign visitors, which is precisely its appeal. The region is also one of the most undeveloped parts of Italy, with a fantastic cuisine and a beautiful landscape. Its coastline hides several fine beaches but the chief pleasures here revolve around meal times and the leisurely Italian pace of life you'll find in the towns and villages.

Over the centuries Puglia has been invaded by most of its neighbours, including Greece and Spain, and you can see these outside influences in many of its towns. Your first step is to base yourself somewhere close to Lecce or Martina Franca, two of the region's most vibrant towns and both close to Brindisi. Lecce has a delightfully over-the-top baroque old town and easy access to the white-sand beaches of the Salentine Peninsula. Martina Franca is one of the livelier towns in Puglia, boasting an annual summer arts festival and a relaxed social scene. Thanks to a mild climate, much of Puglia's socialising takes place out of doors for most of the year.

With an ever-present threat of invasion, Puglia's rulers built some formidable castles and the remnants of these are among the region's highlights. If you have the time, drive to the mysterious 13th-century Castel del Monte in Andria, on the north side of Bari.

Food from Puglia

Strongly influenced by Greek cuisine, from across the Ionian Sea, Puglian cooking is deliciously different. For example, lamb and fish grilled over fires scented with rosemary and thyme is a local favourite. The region produces much of Italy's olive harvest and fresh fish are abundant. Puglia's most distinct pasta is the small orecchiette (*orecchio* is Italian for 'ear') while the best-known cheeses from the region are ricotta and mozzarella. Puglia's cooking, like its wine, can be characterised as being slightly rough-and-ready but no less tasty for it, thanks to the quality of the raw ingredients.

CAGLIARI (SARDINIA)

When the writer D. H. Lawrence set out for Sardinia in his travel book *Sea and Sardinia*, he made sure to pack hot tea and bacon sandwiches. You don't need to take any such precautions these days, the island being such a popular and family-friendly holiday spot. Most visitors will make straight for the Costa Smeralda, an upscale, modern beach resort, but the rest of the island also rewards exploration.

Cagliari, described by Lawrence as 'rising rather bare and proud,' yet, 'jewel-like,' is the island's capital, set in a bay at the south of the island. Cagliari faces Africa and Sardinia is as influenced by North African and Spanish (specifically Catalan) culture as it is by mainland Italy. Cagliari itself, as Lawrence notes, is a fortress, with high castle walls rising from the rocky promontory on which the city was founded. It's Sardinia's biggest and busiest place but the old town centre is still an enjoyable place to wander among 13th-century churches and narrow lanes. At night the locals come out to walk along the Via Manno.

Sardinia is blessed with pristine beaches and seas; the 1,800-kilometre (1,118-mile) long coastline is a mixture of sandy beaches and rocky headlands and cliffs, with some of the best coves to be found south of Cagliari around the Chia Peninsula. Water sports are a big draw here with sailing, diving and windsurfing lessons available at the larger resorts. Inland, the island's landscape is mountainous and rugged with fragrant pine forests where wild flowers bloom in spring. Walkers will love exploring the interior during this time of year.

Alghero

For those in search of more than sun, sea and sand, Sardinia's oldest resort is still its most appealing. This working fishing port has an atmospheric old town centre where the Catalan influence on Sardinia can be clearly seen in the architecture. Alghero's citadel contains a cathedral, two palaces and a theatre behind seven defensive towers – this part of town is pedestrianised. Below the citadel, Alghero's port sees fishing boats landing their catches, some of which go straight to the town's excellent restaurants.

HOW TO GET THERE
easyJet has flights to Cagliari from Luton. Thomsonfly has flights to Alghero from Birmingham and London Gatwick.

CONTACTS/FURTHER INFORMATION
www.comune.cagliari.it

The coastline at Alghero

FLORENCE

HOW TO GET THERE

Meridiana and Alitalia fly direct to Florence; Ryanair, Jet2, easyJet and Thomsonfly fly to Pisa from where there is a frequent train service to Florence.

CONTACTS/FURTHER INFORMATION

www.firenzeturismo.it
www.pisaturismo.it
www.cinqueterre.com

View From San Miniato

Pisa

Served by several low-budget airlines, Pisa is a more usual point of entry to this corner of Tuscany. Of course, the town is more famous for its leaning tower than its airport. Pisa is often visited on a daytrip from Florence but it deserves more. As well as the iconic tower – now shored up for the foreseeable future – Pisa has an outstanding array of sights in the Campo dei Miracoli (the Field of Miracles). Here, the Duomo, Camposanto and Baptistry are a trio of marble-clad masterpieces. The domed Baptistry dates from the 12th century and combines Romanesque and Gothic architecture, while the Duomo pre-dates it by a century.

Florence has cast its spell over artists for centuries, such as two of the world's greatest, Leonardo da Vinci and Michelangelo who competed with each other here. Many years later Florence would also inspire poets, such as Elizabeth Barrett Browning, who is buried in the city's English Cemetery, and novelists like E. M. Forster who set *A Room With A View* here.

The city is the cradle of the Renaissance, the 15th-century cultural movement, and forms part of a Tuscan triangle with Siena and Pisa that is a well-trodden tourist route. There will be crowds throughout the year, although May and September to October are the best months to visit; there is free entry to all state museums in May. This part of Italy is so rich in sights and history that you'll be tempted to explore for much longer than a

> "You can walk between all of Florence's **highlights** in its compact city centre but the busy streets can be a bit of an anticlimax after the **art**."

Leaning Tower, Pisa

weekend. In addition to Pisa and Siena, there is the nearby town of Lucca, a masterpiece of Romanesque architecture that thankfully, receives a fraction of the attention of Florence and Siena. South of Florence are some of Tuscany's wonderful hill-top towns. Often the preserve of regional nobles, these towns are well preserved. The most popular tends to be San Gimignano, with its iconic towers (towers were a sign of a town's prosperity; San Gimignano had 72, of which a dozen remain), although Volterra, its neighbour, is a little-visited gem.

Florence alone, can entertain for days although don't expect to dance the night away; its nightlife is not the best in Italy. The three must-see sights in Florence are the Duomo, Florence's domed cathedral, the Uffizi gallery, guardian of Italy's finest artworks, and the Accademia, home of Michelangelo's *David*. In all three cases, the delights are indoors and you'll have to brave the queues unless you book in advance (recommended). Patience is rewarded at the Uffizi with seeing transcendent art such as Botticelli's *Birth of Venus* and Titian's *Venus of Urbino* in the flesh. Many of the paintings in the gallery were funded by patronage from, at one time, Europe's wealthiest family, the Medici. This Florentine family dominated the city for three centuries, sparking the Renaissance. You can walk between all of Florence's highlights in its compact city centre but the busy streets can be a bit of an anticlimax after the art. A more handsome medieval city lies to the south: Siena. Unlike Florence, you can get the best out of Siena by just absorbing the city from its piazzas, particularly Il Campo.

Cinque Terre

While art-lovers will be craning their necks for a better view of Florence's paintings or Siena's skyline, active types may want to stretch their legs. The Cinque Terre is a group of five coastal villages where Liguria meets Tuscany. These villages – Riomaggiore, Corniglia, Manarola, Monterosso and, arguably the most attractive, Vernazza, are set along a stunning coast of cliffs and coves, much of which is protected by national park status. Cars are banned from the village centres. However, hikers can walk along a special route, the Sentiero Azzurro (the Blue Trail) that connects the five ports with a narrow, 12-kilometre (7-mile) path. Most walkers start in Riomaggiore, breaking their journey as they reach each village along the trail; there's food to be had in all the villages and wines from the terraced vineyards that cling to the steep slopes.

050

HOW TO GET THERE
Jet2, easyJet and Ryanair fly
to Milan from UK airports.

**CONTACTS/FURTHER
INFORMATION**
www.milanoinfotourist.com
www.cenacolovinciano.it
www.teatroallascala.org

Galleria Vittoria Emanuele

MILAN

On the surface, the capital of the northern region of Lombardy might seem to be a brusque, businesslike and determinedly un-Italian city. Commerce is king here, with many of Italy's biggest brands based in Milan, but dig a little deeper and you'll find that Milan's cultural attractions are second to none. Milan has a relatively compact historic core, centred on the Piazza Duomo. Milan's cathedral is one of the largest in the world and is noted for its beautiful, cavernous interior. The Duomo took almost 600 years to complete, which explains its spectrum of architectural styles. There are excellent views of the city from the roof.

But for the best sight in the city, you will have to book in advance and join a group: Leonardo da Vinci's mural of *Cenacolo Vinciano* (*The Last Supper*) is one of the most awe-inspiring works of art in the world and access to the church of Santa Maria delle Grazie, west of the Duomo, has had to be restricted.

Fortunately, if you can't get a space, Milan has several outstanding art galleries and museums. Many of them, including the Pinacoteca Brera, are located in the Brera quarter; this is also the heart of Milan's café society. The most sought-after seat in town, however, is in La Scala, Milan's world-class opera house.

Shopping

Milan is the headquarters of Armani, Prada, Versace and Missoni making it Italy's, if not Europe's, fashion capital. When you've exhausted the boutiques of London and Paris, Milan is the place to turn to. Most of the major fashion houses are represented in the Quadrilatero d'Oro, the gold rectangle formed by the main shopping avenues of Via Montenapoleone and Via della Spiga. On these two parallel streets and in the lanes in between you'll find outlets from Armani, Fendi, Missoni, Paul Smith, Dolce y Gabbana, Prada, Versace and Valentino among others. Those that prefer independent designers to the big labels should head to the Corsa di Porta Ticinese. European department stores are located around Corso Vittoria Emanuele and Via Torino but if you want to save more money, Milan's factory outlets sell complete outfits for the price of a pair of Prada shoes. Many of these discount stores are on the outskirts of the city; the Milan tourist office has a list of outlets, such as Il Salvagente, and how to find them.

NAPLES

'See Naples and die,' goes the saying. And it's true, Naples is a remarkable, mind-boggling city. Unlike some Italian cities such as Bologna or Rome, its Roman sights are spread across the sprawling city although you can limit yourself to the historic centre and still not see everything in a weekend; the Gothic-flavoured Duomo is on the eastern edge of Spaccanapoli, the heart of the Centro Storico around the crossroads of Via San Biagio dei Librai and Via San Gregorio Armeno. South of Spaccanapoli, by the port, is the Palazzo Reale and Castel Nuovo, built in the 13th century, although both are somewhat lost among the noise of this overcrowded city.

Via Toledo is the main shopping street in Naples while nightlife revolves around family-run restaurants (Naples is the spiritual home of the pizza) and bars in the old town such as those around Piazza San Domenico Maggiore. However, you'll need a lot of energy and patience to survive Naples. Take a breather from the city with a daytrip to nearby Pompeii or to the summit of the Roman city's nemesis, Mount Vesuvius.

The Amalfi Coast

South of the Bay of Naples lies one of Italy's most exclusive holiday spots, the Amalfi Coast, where picturesque villages tumble down the cliffs to the sea. The corniche road winds its way past towns that have become sybaritic havens for the Euro-rich: Positano, Sorrento and Ravello. To say it gets congested in the summer would be an understatement. But you can enjoy the Amalfi Coast without booking a luxury hotel or eating at the Michelin-starred restaurants. Even in chic Positano there are good value bed-and-breakfasts; just avoid the over-priced seafront restaurants. Amalfi is perhaps the most convenient base, with a more down-to-earth air than Positano and Ravello. Rather than duelling with thousands of other drivers on the coast ride, you can also tour the Amalfi Coast by boat, stopping at all the major towns.

HOW TO GET THERE
Thomsonfly, Monarch, easyJet, British Airways and MyTravel fly to Naples from airports across the UK.

CONTACTS/FURTHER INFORMATION
www.inaples.it
www.pompeiisites.org

The Bay of Naples and Mount Vesuvius

PALERMO (SICILY)

HOW TO GET THERE
easyJet and Ryanair fly to Palermo; additionally Monarch, Thomsonfly and Thomas Cook Airlines fly to Catania.

CONTACTS/FURTHER INFORMATION
www.apt.catania.it
www.palermotourism.com

Sicilians share their stunning island with two formidable forces: Mount Etna, Europe's most active volcano, and La Cosa Nostra. Impoverished, raw and beautiful, Sicily is an intoxicating place and the Mafia myths add another layer of intrigue. The crime group's power base is in Palermo on the north shore of the island, despite a century of efforts to purge the mobsters from Italy. Art imitates reality in Palermo, where the Teatro Massimo was used in the film *The Godfather III*.

As well as organised crime, Palermo has a reputation for suicidal traffic, decayed and crumbling neighbourhoods and a mix-and-match architectural legacy left by all its invaders, from the Spanish to the Saracens. It's a frenetic place with its sights only rivalled on Sicily by Catania. The highlights are spread across four quarters meeting at the Quattro Canti crossroads. Two of the main attractions date from the Norman conquest of Sicily; the Cattedrale, next to the Capo, Palermo's oldest quarter, and the Palazzo dei Normanni in the Albergheria.

Respite from Palermo's manic pace can be sought in the beach resorts of the east coast. Overshadowed by Mount Etna, Taormina was always the prettiest town in Sicily, although the town and its beaches get overwhelmed with sun seekers from May to September these days. South of Taormina at the base of Mount Etna, Catania is a quieter alternative to Palermo. Its Roman ruins are as well preserved as those of the island's capital and the city has a much more open-minded approach to life than Palermo; you'll find Sicily's best restaurants in Catania and other towns and cities in the southeastern corner of the island rather than the more old-fashioned north and west of Sicily. The local cuisine is superb, based on the freshest possible fish and simple but delicious recipes such as *spaghetti alla Norma*. Explore towns such as Noto on the Ionian coast and Modica for a taste of Sicily at its best. A fiery end to the trip can be had with a fascinating, if slightly nerve-wracking, daytrip from Catania to Mount Etna, Europe's largest and most volatile volcano.

Cathedral

HOW TO GET THERE
Ryanair flies to Parma from
London Stansted.

**CONTACTS/FURTHER
INFORMATION**
www.turismo.comune.parma.it
www.emiliaromagnaturismo.it

Parma shop front

PARMA

You don't have to love food to enjoy Parma but it helps. The city is one of a string set along the Via Emilia in the northern Italian region of Emilia-Romagna, which is sandwiched between Tuscany and Lombardy and is the source of many of Italy's most revered ingredients. The Via Emilia motorway runs from Milan to Rimini and you can almost eat your way along the route: Parma is famous for its prosciutto ham and Parmigiano Reggiano cheese, next Modena produces Italy's best balsamic vinegars, while Bologna is the gastronomic capital of Italy.

Parma itself is a large town of 170,000 inhabitants. It's a sedate, affluent place with a handsome medieval core built around the Piazza Garibaldi and the Duomo, and a highbrow cultural scene with busy opera and theatre seasons at the main opera house, Teatro Regio and the Teatro Due on the riverfront.

But Parma's best performances take place in its restaurants, delicatessens and markets. This is where the region's superlative ingredients take centre stage to wow their public.

Real Parmesan

A wedge of hard, aged Parmigiano Reggiano from Emilia-Romagna bears no relation to the flavourless packets of Parmesan cheese typically sold in supermarkets. The real version of Parmesan has been around for thousands of years. It's a durable, matured cheese that improves anything to which it is added; Italian climbers will often pack a chunk in their backpacks and waiters shave off slivers into customers' pasta. True Parmigiano Reggiano is a carefully protected product; its milk can only come from a restricted area of Emilia-Romagna where the cows have to be fed on a special diet. The cheese-making season runs from April to November. The cheeses are formed into huge wheels weighing 35 kilograms (77 pounds) and aged for up to four years. Those that pass inspection are marked with a series of dots.

PERUGIA

HOW TO GET THERE
Ryanair flies to Perugia from
London Stansted.

**CONTACTS/FURTHER
INFORMATION**
www.sangallo.it/umbria

Perugia at sunset

Umbria has already been nominated as the next Tuscany, the region on its northern border. However, Umbria is a big place and the overflow of visitors from Tuscany hasn't yet spoiled this peaceful, rustic region where the natural and the man-made seem to exist in harmony. Umbria's capital is the city of Perugia, which beneath its rather plain exterior has some interesting ruins that tell how the Etruscans – a sophisticated pre-Roman civilisation that settled in most of western Italy – forced out the local people: they were later conquered by the Romans. Perugia is organised around the broad Corso Vannucci; start the day with a cappuccino at one of its cafés while watching life ebb and flow along the street. At the far end of Corso Vannucci, the Piazza IV Novembre is the focal point for Perugia's student nightlife, with bars and restaurants, plus Perugia's Duomo. Opposite the Duomo is the Palazzo dei Priori, an imposing palace open to the public and containing medieval frescoes. More frescoes, by the local artist Pietro Vannucci, can be seen further down Corso Vannucci in the Collegio di Cambio, the city's old money exchange.

But to get a true sense of Umbria's art and history, you'll have to leave Perugia and visit some of the nearby medieval hilltop towns. The town of Assisi is just a short drive east from Perugia (and there are regular buses). As the birthplace of Italy's most well-known saint, St Francis of Assisi, born in 1182, it attracts a large number of pilgrims. They come to see the Basilica di San Francesco, Umbria's most impressive attraction. The shrine, its interior layered with frescoes, contains one of the most fascinating art exhibitions outside a gallery and anyone with an interest in Italian art will enjoy seeing the progression in style and technique through the ages, the summit of the collection being work by Simone Martini and Pietro Lorenzetti. St Francis is buried in the basilica's crypt.

Make your way north for Umbria's best medieval town, Gubbio. Without a saint of its own, it doesn't have the footfall of Assisi, but it does have the best-preserved medieval centre of any Umbrian town.

" **To get a true sense of Umbria's art and history, you'll have to leave Perugia and visit some of the nearby medieval hilltop towns.** "

RIMINI

The seaside resort of Rimini, birthplace of film director Federio Fellini, and its smaller sibling to the south, Riccione, attracts young Italians from all over the country with its blend of nightclubs, beaches and 24-hour entertainment. Best described as the Blackpool of Italy, Rimini has a 14-kilometre (9-mile) seafront promenade lined with clubs playing house music all night; revellers can tumble straight onto the rather lacklustre sands of the Adriatic coast. There's a sleazy edge to parts of Rimini that families should be aware of. After all, it was in a Rimini hotel room that Italian cyclist Marco Pantani died after a cocaine overdose in 2004. For a more upmarket time, continue 16 kilometres (10 miles) south to Riccione, a smaller town with an equally vibrant club scene. This unsung area of Italy has been attracting holidaying racing cyclists for six years now, thanks to Riccione Bike Hotels, who provide maps, food, workshops and guides. The initiative aims to replicate the success Mallorca has enjoyed in attracting cyclists in the off-peak seasons (March to May, September to November). Pantani lived, trained and died in this small area of the Emilia Romagna region and many cyclists travel to Riccione to follow in his tyre tracks. Another local hero is motorcycle racer Valentino Rossi from Tavullia.

Urbino

With a university that is more than 500 years old and a reputation for culture established by the city's founder, Renaissance man Federico da Montefeltro, Urbino is a highly-recommended antidote to Rimini's hedonism. The hilltop fortress is located inland from Pésaro in the rural, undeveloped Marche region. It's the highlight of the area and an afternoon can be wiled away in the sun-kissed piazzas of its honey-coloured old town with a coffee and pastries. This part of Urbino is dominated by the Palazzo Ducale, the match of any Tuscan palace, and the city's Duomo. But the rest of the walled quarter is much more lively and the bars and cafés are bustling with young people during term time.

HOW TO GET THERE
Easyjet, Mytravel and Ryanair fly to Rimini from UK airports.

CONTACTS/FURTHER INFORMATION
www.emiliaromagnaturismo.it,
www.riminiturismo.it

Urbino

ROME

HOW TO GET THERE
easyJet, bmibaby, Ryanair, Jet2 and British Airways fly from UK airports.

CONTACTS/FURTHER INFORMATION
www.romaturismo.it
www.vatican.va

Rome, like all major cities, is a work in progress. Fortunately, it has been served well by the last 2,000 years. Rome overwhelms from the moment you set foot in the city. Some of the world's oldest and most dramatic sights are part of the city's fabric – the Pantheon, the Colosseum and the Forum. These monumental buildings were at the heart of ancient Rome, when the Roman Republic was the most powerful force in the world. The River Tiber bisects the Italian capital; the Vatican City is on the west bank while most of Rome's other major sights are in a compact, hilly area on the east bank.

The machinations of Roman politics resembled a soap opera; in 44 BC its most famous ruler, Julius Caesar was stabbed in the back in the Senate, part of the Roman Forum opposite the

Café patio

Ponza

Where do the Romans go in the summer? They head for Ponza, a tiny volcanic island in the Tyrrhenian Sea between Rome and Naples. The island is an almost exclusively Italian getaway, reached by hydrofoil from Anzio. The island's crenellated coastline is washed by an azure sea – sea caves, cliffs and creeks perfect for snorkelling abound although beaches are in short supply. The neighbouring island of Palmarolo, a speck in the sea reached by day-tripper boats from Ponza Town, is even more dreamlike; there are palm trees, a small restaurant and not much else. Ponza clings onto a simple but elegant way of life, which is why it is the favoured port of call of Rome's elite.

The Colosseum

Colosseum, both open to visitors daily. The Colosseum itself was where more than 70,000 Romans could be entertained at a time with often blood-soaked games involving wild animals and gladiators. Although just a shell remains, the Colosseum is an awesome prospect and a fascinating insight into the Roman world.

The Pantheon, in the Centro Storico (historic centre) to the northwest of the Colosseum, is a much more complete Roman ruin. Originally a temple, the perfectly proportioned Pantheon would have been lavishly decorated with frescoes and statues.

To attempt to see all Rome's sights in a weekend would be a Herculean task. As well as the Roman ruins, there are churches with more amazing art than some galleries at every turn, and palaces, piazzas and museums galore. Rome isn't resting on its laurels; a new crop of museums, including the National Museum of 21st Century Arts (Maxxi), and Rome's new Auditorium, which opened in 2002, are often free to visitors. While you can get around the relatively compact centre on foot, there are trams and buses so staying in the outskirts isn't the end of the world. Nightlife in Rome is improving; there are many restaurants in the Centro Storico but bars and clubs tend to be scattered around the city's neighbourhoods; however, live performances – from music to theatre and opera – lag behind many other European capitals. But when most people will be footsore from climbing the Spanish Steps and frolicking around the Trevi Fountain, that's not such a serious shortcoming.

The Vatican

A city within a city, the Vatican, ruled by the Pope, is the centre of the Catholic world and home to 1,000 people, making it the world's smallest independent state. Although the audiences with the Pope in the Piazza San Pietro, plus several other religious events, draw many people to the city, it is the Vatican's astounding museums that inspire the most awe: here are some of the world's greatest artworks, from Renaissance masterpieces to Etruscan relics. Undoubtedly, Michelangelo's ceiling frescoes depicting Creation and the Last Judgement in the Sistine Chapel are the Vatican's star attraction but if you can't afford the time to wait in line, try the sculptures of the Braccio Nuovo or the paintings of the Raphael Stanze – you'll never see it all in a day.

057

HOW TO GET THERE
MyTravel, easyJet, Ryanair and British Airways have flights to Turin from several UK airports including London and Bristol.

CONTACTS/FURTHER INFORMATION
www.turismotorino.org
www.slowfood.com
www.museoauto.it

Turin Tunnel

TURIN

Tucked away in the northwest corner of Italy, Turin is one of Italy's most underrated cities. But it has much going for it. In preceding decades, Turin was an industrial powerhouse and the headquarters of Fiat and other engineering firms. Turin's love affair with the automobile is best expressed in the 1969 film *The Italian Job*, which is as much about the cars as the heist. The test track on top of the Lingotto factory building (now a shopping centre, hotel and modern exhibition centre among other things) featured in the film still stands. As Turin's manufacturing heyday faded, the city began to reinvent itself. It had one very famous attraction – the Turin Shroud – but that could only be displayed every 25 years.

Instead, Turin won the right to host the 2006 Winter Olympics, highlighting how close the city was to superb winter sports amenities. Money was poured into Turin's transport and tourism infrastructure and new sports facilities were constructed. The city, which was the capital of Italy until 1870, has been on the up ever since. You can still get to grips with Turin's automotive past at the comprehensive Museo dell'Automobile and its fabulous collection of Ferraris and Maseratis. But the city also attracts foodie pilgrims to its great restaurants. Turin is the home of the Slow Food movement and a city where shops and restaurants are accredited by the Maestri del Gusto ('Masters of Taste') to sell the very best Piedmontese specialities.

Piedmont

Turin is the gateway to the Piedmont, a rural backwater that has escaped the fate of Tuscany and Umbria and remains a hardworking, agricultural region. Here, hilltop towns are famed for their wines produced by the surrounding vineyards, especially in the mist-shrouded Langhe area. The most attractive town in the Langhe is Alba, which hosts an annual truffle festival celebrating Piedmont's other speciality, the white truffle. Some of Italy's most highly rated wines are from the Piedmont, including rich, luxurious Barolo and Barbaresco, using the local Nebbiolo grape. Unlike the Napa Valley or Bordeaux, wine-tasting tours in the Piedmont need to be arranged in advance (or go with an organised tour). The vineyard owners are invariably welcoming and very hospitable.

VENICE

For centuries, Venice has sent poets and artists from Byron to Turner into raptures. They loved the city as much for its unique layout on 100 islands as for its impressive cultural heritage. Gazing down the Grand Canal from the Rialto Bridge or crossing the Piazza San Marco in a flurry of pigeons are some of the once-in-a-lifetime experiences that Venice has to offer. But beware: Venice is one of very few European cities where demand exceeds supply. The city is packed to bursting point during the summer and hoteliers can charge exorbitant rates. Restaurants are similarly overpriced; it's one of the few places in Italy where good, basic meals are hard to come by. The best advice is to visit out of the peak season and, with gondola rides costing over 70 euros an hour, forget living on a tight budget.

Start the weekend with a *vaporetti* (water bus) ride down the length of the Grand Canal – this will give you an idea of the layout of Venice. Smaller canals are offshoots from the Grand Canal and will lead to quieter sights such as the Campo dei Frari, a wonderful Gothic church with a work by Titian hung over its altar. A much wider collection of Titians and other Venetian art can be viewed in the Galleria dell'Accademia. Combining soaring Venetian-Gothic architecture with more frescoes by Tintoretto, the Palazzo Ducale is in the Piazza San Marco. Also in the Piazza is Caffe Florian, so old that Byron himself drank here. Venice becomes much more comfortable if money is no object; drink bellinis at Henry's Bar on Calle Vallaresso and eat at Da Fiore on Calle del Scalater. Then, if there's time, hop on a vaporetti to the lagoon's islands: atmospheric Torcello and Murano, famous for glass-blowing.

"**Also in the Piazza is Caffe Florian, so old that Byron himself drank here.**"

HOW TO GET THERE
easyJet, Jet2, Monarch, Thomsonfly, Ryanair and Thomsonfly fly to Venice from various UK airports. British Airways also has a regular service.

FURTHER INFORMATION
www.turismovenezia.it

Gondolier at sunset

059

VERONA

HOW TO GET THERE
British Airways, Ryanair and
Thomas Cook Airlines fly to
Verona.

**CONTACTS/FURTHER
INFORMATION**
www.tourism.verona.it
www.trentino.to

Mountain biker in the Dolomites

The one-time Roman city of Verona is best known for being the setting of Shakespeare's *Romeo and Juliet*, but there is much more to the city than just its famous balcony. With Roman sights to rival those of Venice, Verona's visitors should make time for the city's Arena (the third largest amphitheatre in Italy) and the Roman theatre on the other side of the River Adige. Many of Verona's finest buildings date from the 12th and 13th centuries when the city was a regional power. The central piazzas are where many of the city's restaurants and shops are located now and are far better value than those of Venice.

"**Ski resorts in the Dolomites** such as Cortina d'Ampezzo can offer better value **skiing** than the Alps"

Adventure in the Dolomites

A weekend in the northern Italian region of Trentino, north of Verona, can be as action-packed as you like. The combination of the Dolomites mountain range and water sports on Lake Garda mean that a wide range of adventures are on your doorstep. At the north tip of Lake Garda, Torbole and Riva del Garda are mountain-biking meccas; more than 7,000 kilometres (4,350 miles) of forest tracks are open to bikers and bike shops can provide detailed maps. Much of the mountain biking around Lake Garda is all about ferocious climbs and steep, technical descents, the most notorious of which is called Tremalzo – you'll shoot through wartime tunnels carved into solid rock and past sheer cliffs over the lake. Motorboats are banned on all of Trentino's 297 lakes, so windsurfing has really taken off at the northern end of Lake Garda. Better still, the 'Ora' breeze picks up at 1pm. Inland from Riva del Garda, the town of Arco has become a world-class adventure sports hotspot, with climbers in particular travelling from all over the world to try the region's rock faces: there is something for rock climbers of all abilities, with single and multi-pitch routes. The tourist office in Arco and the Trentino Mountain Climbing Association can provide more information. Note that it can be too hot to climb in mid-summer. In the winter, ski resorts in the Dolomites such as Cortina d'Ampezzo can offer better value skiing than the Alps, although the snow may be patchier.

LATVIA

Latvia is a small country set on the shore of the Baltic Sea, nestled between Lithuania and Estonia. Its capital, Riga, is something of a hybrid. Lacking the quaint medieval core of the Estonian capital Tallinn, Riga is as austerely handsome as the Swedish capital Stockholm across the sea, with an added twist of art nouveau elegance. It survived years of Soviet control and now enjoys its status as a UNESCO World Heritage site. The rest of the country, with a population of 2.2 million, is largely flat, with river floodplains and photogenic castles.

TIME DIFFERENCE GMT +2 (Central European Summer Time +3)

TELEPHONE CODE +371

CURRENCY Lats

LANGUAGE Latvian

NATIONAL TRANSPORT WEBSITE www.ldz.lv

POPULATION 2,200,000

SIZE OF COUNTRY 63,700 sq km (24,595 sq m)

CAPITAL Riga

WHEN TO GO Prime time in Latvia is either the height of summer – when the sun is out and the weather is hot with very long daylight hours – or the depths of winter when Riga becomes a fairytale-perfect city with snow-capped roofs and Christmas lights. Spring and autumn tend to be damp and disappointing in comparison.

TOURIST INFORMATION www.latviatourism.lv

HOW TO GET THERE
Easyjet and Ryanair have flights from London airports to Riga.

CONTACTS/FURTHER INFORMATION
www.latviatourism.lv
www.sigulda.lv

The historic centre of the city

RIGA

Times have changed since Riga's tourist board proclaimed that 'canned sprats' were one of the Latvian capital's chief attractions. Latvia joined the EU in 2004 and is one of a trio of post-Communist Baltic states grasping the opportunities of capitalism with both hands. Tourism is booming and the city has become a fixture on the stag party circuit, in part thanks to cheap beer and a no-holds-barred nightlife.

But look beyond the bars and the Soviet-era concrete blocks in the suburbs and you'll find a colourful city centre rich in history and art. The old town itself has UNESCO World Heritage status thanks to buildings dating from the city's foundation in 1201 and an unparalleled art nouveau neighbourhood that was once home to Isaiah Berlin. The 700-year old Dome cathedral is one of the city's landmarks but there are several fascinating museums too, dealing with the Soviet and Nazi occupation of Riga and how the country's Jewish population fared.

Riga is changing fast; enjoy it now.

Extreme Sports in Latvia

Adventures in Latvia are not limited to Riga's nightlife; 48 kilometres (30 miles) northeast of Riga is the country's main hub for adventure sports, Sigulda (there is a direct train service and driving there will take about an hour). This mountain town is the gateway to the Gauya National Park. In winter this is the principal spot for winter sports while in the summer the River Gauya becomes the centre of attention for canoeists and kayakers. The river flows through deep sandstone gorges and you can camp along its length. Keep an eye out for the wildlife: peregrines in the sky, trout, salmon and otters in the river. Even wilder, Sigulda boasts an Olympic standard bobsleigh track. It is one of the few tracks that allow members of the public to test their nerve against the clock and gravity. In the summer the bobsleigh runs on wheels but in the winter the track is clad in ice.

LITHUANIA

Lithuania, like its diminutive neighbour Latvia, joined the EU in 2004, although the country has always enjoyed tighter ties with its neighbour to the south, Poland. The capital, Vilnius, is in the flatlands of the very south of the country. With an amazingly well preserved historic core – one of the largest in Europe – this is a city that repays several days of exploration. When you're not sightseeing, the fantastic bars and restaurants of Vilnius will tempt even the most experienced hedonist.

TIME DIFFERENCE GMT +2 (Central European Summer Time +3)

TELEPHONE CODE +370

CURRENCY Litas

LANGUAGE Lithuanian

NATIONAL TRANSPORT WEBSITE www.litrail.lt

POPULATION 3,400,000

SIZE OF COUNTRY 65,200 sq km (25,174 sq m)

CAPITAL Vilnius

WHEN TO GO Lithuania has a short but bright summer. The mid-winter is a dark and cold time of year. Spring and autumn are highly variable.

061

VILNIUS

HOW TO GET THERE
AirBaltic flies to Vilnius from London Gatwick; Ryanair flies to Lithuania's second city, Kaunas.

CONTACTS/FURTHER INFORMATION
www.turizmas.vilnius.lt

Vilnius Old Town

Lithuania is one of a triumvirate of Baltic states that have embraced capitalism since joining the EU in 2004. But Lithuania's capital, Vilnius, differs from Riga and Tallinn in several subtle ways. Firstly, it is a couple of hundred miles from the Baltic sea and the city has traditionally had closer links with Russia and Poland to the south than its sister states to the north. Secondly, Vilnius doesn't pop up on the radar of stag parties as readily as Tallinn and is an altogether quieter proposition.

Yet the Lithuanian capital does have some things in common with Tallinn: it too is an extraordinarily beautiful city with a compact and delightfully medieval Old Town. At every turn of the cobbled lanes there is a bijou square or a baroque church, such as the extravagant St Peter and St Paul church, or the church of St Anne, which looks as if it was designed after a night of absinthe drinking, a popular spirit in the bars of the Old Town. Thankfully, the architectural legacy of the Soviet occupation is much less apparent here than in many other Eastern European cities.

Most visitors stay in the Old Town; it is where most of the hotels, museums and restaurants are located. Restaurants in Vilnius have become much more adventurous since the retreat of Communism and it is possible to find Nordic, Greek and French food, although don't overlook traditional Lithuanian restaurants if you're looking for a large, filling meal. Similarly, the arts are also resurgent in Vilnius. There are small galleries in the Uzupis quarter, across the River Vilnia and the Museum of Applied Art in the Old Town will occupy a couple of hours. However, the one must-see attraction is the KGB Museum.

Other excursions should include taking the funicular railway to the top of Castle Hill for views over Vilnius or planning a daytrip to the Island Castle at Trakai.

LUXEMBOURG

What Luxembourg lacks in size – this is a true European city-state – it more than makes up for with an appetite for good living. The city is one of the best in Europe for dining out (this may or may not have anything to do with the resident Eurocrats and bankers) but its beautiful location may also surprise first-time visitors. Tucked into a nook between northern France, Germany and Belgium, Luxembourg is at the heart of Western Europe, with the galleries and museums of a much larger nation. Accessible, pleasurable and full of treats, Luxembourg deserves a closer look.

TIME DIFFERENCE GMT +1 (Central European Summer Time +2)

TELEPHONE CODE +352

CURRENCY Euro

LANGUAGE French, German and Luxembourgish

NATIONAL TRANSPORT WEBSITE www.cfl.lu

POPULATION 460,000

SIZE OF COUNTRY 2,586 sq km (998 sq m)

CAPITAL Luxembourg

WHEN TO GO With Luxembourg's strengths being its restaurants and sights, rather than outdoor activities, the weather need not play a large part in your plans. Being a low-lying city, it's not forbiddingly cold in winter and has a long, warm summer.

TOURIST INFORMATION www.lcto.lu

HOW TO GET THERE
LuxAir, VLM and British Airways from various London airports and Manchester; TGV train direct from Paris (journey time: two hours)

CONTACTS/FURTHER INFORMATION
www.lcto.lu

Abaye Neumünster

LUXEMBOURG

Luxembourg, like Zurich, has suffered from the perception that it is nothing more than a dormitory for an army of overpaid bankers. Yes, Luxembourg is certainly one of the wealthiest cities in Europe – attracting the moderately wealthy rather than the super-rich – but it is in the process of putting that money to good use.

As well as grand restaurants – Luxembourg boasts more Michelin-starred restaurants per person than anywhere else – the city is fast becoming as well known for its appreciation of art as rich food. So much so, in fact, that Luxembourg was declared the European Capital of Culture for 2007.

Recent examples of Luxembourg's zeal for art include the Museum of Modern Art, which was designed by architect I. M. Pei and opened in 2006, and the Natural History and Art Museum, which was revamped in 2002, and a defiantly modern concert hall, the venue for many of Luxembourg's frequent arts festivals.

Another surprise might be Luxembourg's setting. This is no faceless, modern metropolis; the 1,000-year-old city perches above deep, rocky ravines among forest-clad hillsides. With amazing views from the city's balustrades,

Luxembourg is made for exploring on foot: there is a Saturday market in the Place Guillaume, a grand palace and the city's own castle, dating from 963 and now a UNESCO World Heritage site.

Clean, safe and compact, Luxembourg is a well-kept secret at the crossroads of Europe.

The Museum of Modern Art

I.M. Pei's brutally geometric design for this outstanding museum would have required extensive use of the set square and ruler. A white-walled obelisk that stands in steadfast contrast to the spindly spires of Luxembourg's Gothic churches and the bourgeois, honey-coloured townhouses, the museum, informally known as the MUDAM, will excite anyone with an appetite for modern architecture. The project cost 90 million euros and is one of Europe's leading museums of modern art. Everything from photography and multimedia to painting and fashion is exhibited.

NETHERLANDS

This famously liberal country has a distinct national character – but it's not that which most people see when they visit Amsterdam. Rather than the 'anything-goes' antics of the Dutch capital, the Netherlands is actually a rather strait-laced, sober place thanks to a strain of strict Protestantism that still influences town and village society. So, it is all the stranger that Amsterdam can provide experiences to visitors that are illegal in their home countries. Beyond the famous coffeeshops, however, the Dutch capital is a beautiful, waterborne city with some of the finest art galleries in Europe.

TIME DIFFERENCE GMT +1 (Central European Summer Time +2)

TELEPHONE CODE +31

CURRENCY Euro

LANGUAGE Dutch

NATIONAL TRANSPORT WEBSITE www.ns.nl

POPULATION 16,300,000

SIZE OF COUNTRY 41,526 sq km (16,033 sq m)

CAPITAL Amsterdam

WHEN TO GO Winter is generally wet and grey in the Netherlands but spring brings blooms of flowers (such as the famous tulip fields). At the end of April, Koninginnedag (Queen's Day) is an extremely popular day of festivities when accommodation will be fully booked in advance. Summer and early autumn are pleasant times of the year to visit.

TOURIST INFORMATION www.holland.com

063

HOW TO GET THERE
easyJet, Thomsonfly and Jet2
fly to Amsterdam from several
UK cities.

**CONTACTS/FURTHER
INFORMATION**
www.visitamsterdam.nl

An Amsterdam canal

AMSTERDAM

The Dutch city of Amsterdam has suffered unfairly from stereotyping. If it's not people sniggering about the famous red-light district – which is retained for the benefit of tourist photo opportunities – they're asking about the coffeeshops that sell cannabis alongside espressos or conjuring up images of windmills and bicycles. Perhaps the city needs to remind the world that it is home to some of the most extraordinary collections of fine art in Europe and some of the continent's prettiest urban landscapes.

Amsterdam's golden age began in the late 16th century when Dutch banking practices were revolutionising the way wars and trade were funded. Through trade and loans, Amsterdam thrived, sometimes through risky sleights of hand. An example: cash loaned from Amsterdam banks paid the wages of Spanish soldiers while timber from Amsterdam's merchants built the Spanish navy – all of which guaranteed the Dutch city immunity from attack by the marauding Spanish armies. Freight and shipbuilding were also counted among the city's strengths, until England started flexing its muscles in the 17th century. Amsterdam went into decline throughout the 18th century but the city had already established itself as a cosmopolitan but pragmatic place. A new ingredient, liberalism, seeped into the

Amsterdam character from the 1960s to the 1990s, resulting in a city where pretty much anything goes, within reason.

Any tour of Amsterdam should begin back in the 19th century, in the leafy district known as the Museum Quarter, where wealthy landowners had built grand mansions surrounded by gardens and parks. Here, today, are some of Amsterdam's world-class museums: the Rijksmuseum's restoration is scheduled to conclude in 2009 but you can still see work by Vermeer, Rembrandt and other Dutch masters as well as a wide selection of exhibits from doll's houses to porcelain. Here, too, is the Van Gogh Museum, laid out chronologically, and, for fans of modern art, the Stedelijk Museum, which contains an extraordinary and eclectic collection of sculpture, painting and photography by artists from Picasso to Warhol.

While Amsterdam has always attracted hipsters, it can be hard avoiding the herds of coach parties. Fortunately, while Amsterdam's centre is diminutive and dominated by Rembrandtplein, it is easy to follow one of the canals out to less-frequented neighbourhoods such as Jordaan and Prinsengracht. These neighbourhoods show off the best of Amsterdam with flower-decked bridges and buildings lit up at night and plenty of chic bars and restaurants to try. Not even the city's infamous coffeeshops are as intoxicating as a late-night stroll beside these canals.

As Amsterdam aims to attract the well-heeled visitor, so more tempting boutiques and shops open. One of the best shopping districts is the Nine Streets area, between the Singel and Prinsengracht canals – the emphasis here is on funky independent outlets. There are better cities for department stores but Amsterdam is a haven for the entrepreneur. And, without perpetuating another Dutch cliché, one speedy way of seeing Amsterdam is by hiring a bicycle.

Rotterdam

The Dutch city of Rotterdam is the sci-fi alter-ego of twee Amsterdam. The southern city, close to Utrecht, is an industrial port but thanks to some stellar modern architecture and the most upbeat nightlife in the Netherlands it is an exciting place to visit for a day or two. The city was razed to the ground during the Second World War so planners and architects had a blank slate for Rotterdam's reconstruction. The resulting metropolis was the 2007 City of Architecture. One of the highlights of the city is the angular suspension bridge running from north to south, the iconic Erasmus Bridge. But at every turn you will see soaring, modern buildings; the city is home to the Netherlands Architecture Institute, which is worth a look, as is the Nederland's Fotomuseum, which relocated to an exciting new building in 2007. But you don't have to be an architecture student to enjoy Rotterdam. The city's residents have an unsurpassed appetite for dance music and every weekend 10,000 clubbers hit the city's dance floors. The soundtrack varies from funky house music to pounding hard techno, making the city second only to Berlin for lovers of electronic music. Rotterdam is a 45-minute train journey from Amsterdam.

Amsterdam architecture

064 DELFT

HOW TO GET THERE
KLM fly from London to Rotterdam. Take a train from Rotterdam to Delft (journey time is 10 minutes).

CONTACTS/FURTHER INFORMATION
www.delft.nl

Delft canal

This charming Dutch city is one of the best preserved in the Netherlands and closely associated with the Dutch Royal Family. Close to The Hague and Rotterdam, it makes for a rewarding daytrip from either of those cities. Delft has played a key role in Dutch history, being the 16th-century home of William of Orange. A later resident, in the 17th century, was Johannes Vermeer, now recognised as one of the greatest Dutch painters. Three key sites in the city are related to the Royal Family and Vermeer: the Oude Kerk (the old church), the Nieuwe Kerk (the new church) and the Prinsenhof, a royal palace now used as a museum. The Prinsenhof was William of Orange's residence and you can still see the bullet holes in the wall where he was murdered in 1584. The Royal Family's vaults are in the Nieuwe Kerk while Vermeer is buried in the Oude Kerk. History aside, most people will visit Delft to buy some of the city's famous blue-and-white porcelain, known as delftware. From its height in the 17th century, when 32 factories produced the ceramics, just three remain, all offering guided tours. The Royal Delft factory is the only one to have survived since the 17th century; don't expect any bargains in the factory shops.

The Hague

Some of Johannes Vermeer's most impressive depictions of his home town can be seen in the Mauritshuis Gallery in The Hague, the base for the Dutch government, although the capital of the Netherlands is Amsterdam. The Hague doesn't suffer the same weight of numbers as Amsterdam's great museums, giving you more time and space to appreciate masterpieces by Vermeer such as *Girl With A Pearl Earring*. No artist captured the wan light of Delft as deftly as Vermeer and his *View of Delft* in the Mauritshuis is a tantalising taster of the town. Art lovers should combine a trip to Delft with a stop in The Hague; The Hague City Card offers discounted public transport and admission prices in Delft.

NORWAY

Blessed with a coastline that runs the length of the Scandinavian Peninsula, Norway shelters Sweden from the worst of the North Sea's weather fronts. When it's not raining, however, the Norwegian fjords are astonishingly beautiful and unspoiled places to visit. Bergen, to the southwest of the country is the gateway to the great outdoors and you could easily spend weeks here and still feel like you haven't scraped the surface: like many rugged towns, its character changes according to different weather. Norway's capital, Oslo, offers similarly gripping weekending options but on a city-sized scale.

TIME DIFFERENCE
GMT +1 (Central European Summer Time +2)

TELEPHONE CODE +47

CURRENCY Krone

LANGUAGE Norwegian

NATIONAL TRANSPORT WEBSITE www.nsb.no

POPULATION 4,700,000

SIZE OF COUNTRY 323,878 sq km (125,050 sq m)

CAPITAL Oslo

WHEN TO GO Depending upon your latitude, winters can be exceptionally harsh in Norway, which is why most of the major cities are to be found in the milder south of the country. The high plateaus of the interior offer superb cross-country skiing although beware the short days. In the absence of any outstanding Christmas festivals, most visitors choose to arrive from late spring (May) until early autumn (October). Summers can have long, hot days, perfect for the outdoor activities around Bergen.

TOURIST INFORMATION www.visitnorway.com

065

Fly to Bergen with SAS Braathens from several British cities including London, Manchester, Leeds, Newcastle, Birmingham, Edinburgh, Glasgow and Aberdeen. Flights may be direct or via Copenhagen. Wideroe fly direct to Bergen from Aberdeen and Edinburgh. You can also take a train direct from Oslo to Bergen across central Norway, which is one of the world's greatest train trips.

CONTACTS/FURTHER INFORMATION
www.visitbergen.com

The Bryggen

BERGEN

Bergen, on the fractured west coast of Norway, is the gateway to the country's famous fjords. Although the city has expanded over the years from its origins as a trading and fishing port, it retains the quaint and attractive clapboard buildings that have led the centre to be granted UNESCO World Heritage status. The wooden old town is 700 years old and you can learn about Bergen's history in the Hanseatic Museum. Even in the rain, which feeds the region's spectacular waterfalls, the city is certainly one of the most charming in Europe. It's a great base for exploring the fjords, the best of which are Hardangerfjord to the south and Sognefjord and Nordfjord to the north. Spring, which touches Bergen's fruit trees and rhododendrons in late May and June, is the best time to visit but winter, for sports such as cross-country skiing, is also popular. As always, however, the simplest pleasures are sometimes the best: spend time in Bergen with a coffee at a café on the quayside, watching the boats put-put in and out of the harbour. Just remember to bring a waterproof.

Voss

About 96 kilometres (60 miles) east of Bergen is Norway's rugged adventure playground, Voss. The town, surrounded by mountains and fjords has two claims to fame: it hosts the world's biggest annual extreme sports festival and it is the world capital of base jumping, where daredevils jump off cliffs and bridges. Norway is one of the few countries in the world where this daring variant of parachuting is legal. But you don't have to be a base jumper to enjoy this adrenaline-charged town – even breathing in the zingy sea air is enough to send tingles down your spine. Plenty of tour operators in Voss offer less life-threatening adventure activities, from white-water kayaking to mountain biking. Bergen and Voss are a quirky, though no less expensive, alternative to other Alpine resorts, such as Chamonix.

OSLO

The Norwegian capital is unlikely to feature in a list of low-budget breaks – it is one of the world's most expensive cities. However, there are ways of enjoying this sophisticated and smart city without breaking the bank.

Oslo, like most Norwegian cities, is surrounded by forests, mountains and lakes and with fresh air and sunshine freely available it is possible to tour the surrounding fjords in a ferry or just relax outdoors for very little expense – most public transport, including ferries is included in Oslo's City Pass, a must for sightseers. The Bygdoy Peninsula has a pair of enthralling museums closely connected to Norway's seafaring traditions: the Kon-Tiki Museum, which catalogues adventurer Thor Heyerdahl's expeditions, and the Viking Ship Museum.

In the city centre, there are further bargains to be found indoors. Oslo's National Gallery is free and houses some of the works of Norway's most famous son, Edvard Munch. His painting, *The Scream*, is once again the star attraction of the Edvard Munch Museum after being brazenly stolen in 2004.

What really depletes the wallet, however, is eating and drinking out in the city's bars and restaurants, where a beer can cost £5 and a two-course meal about £50. The Norwegians have developed a tactic to overcome the high prices; they congregate in public places such as the open-air Vigeland Sculpture Park to quaff a few beers and have a snack before hitting the city's nightspots. Vigeland, named after Oslo's celebrated sculptor Gustav Vigeland, lies to the northeast of the city and has barbeque pits and seating for just such activities, where you'll be overlooked by Vigeland's giant stone figures. Of course, this suggestion only applies to fair weather visitors – winters in Oslo are unremittingly harsh with temperatures averaging -5–0°C (23–32°F). To return to the city from Vigeland, walk down the main avenue of the Majorstuen district – the main shopping area in Oslo, its boutiques try to tempt window-shoppers inside with candlelit displays.

HOW TO GET THERE
British Airways and SAS Braathens fly direct to Oslo from London. Ryanair's service to Oslo arrives at Oslo Torp airport, one and a half hours from the city itself.

CONTACTS/FURTHER INFORMATION
www.visitoslo.com

Norwegian Fjord

POLAND

TIME DIFFERENCE GMT +1 (Central European Summer Time +2)

TELEPHONE CODE +48

CURRENCY Zloty

LANGUAGE Polish

NATIONAL TRANSPORT WEBSITE
www.pkp.com.pl

POPULATION 38,000,000

SIZE OF COUNTRY 312,683 sq km (120,728 sq m)

CAPITAL Warsaw

WHEN TO GO The Polish winter is unforgiving, with very low temperatures, although you will find the country's small-scale ski resorts open for business. Otherwise, late May until September is the best time for visiting, should you wish to avoid July and August, which are the busiest months.

TOURIST INFORMATION www.poland.travel

This colossal country has flourished since establishing Eastern Europe's first post-Communist government. It joined the EU in 2004, bringing much needed investment into the country but also an exodus of young workers. At the centre of the country, a trio of cities can be counted among the continent's most fascinating: the capital, Warsaw, Krakow and Wroclaw. Suffusing all of them is Poland's turbulent and sometimes troubled history, not least because of its position wedged between Germany and the old Soviet Union. The character and traditions of the Polish people shine on, however, and their cities are great places to visit as they adapt to a new future.

GDANSK/SOPOT/GDYNIA

This trio of cities lie next to each other on Poland's Baltic coast. They have been described as the Polish Riviera, although that's probably being rather generous to the Baltic climate; although this said, during the hot summers temperatures can hit 30ºC (86ºF). The largest of the three is Gdansk, Poland's main port and the city most closely associated with the Solidarity movement led by Lech Walesa that brought about the first post-Communist elections in Eastern Europe, in 1989. However, while the city has an industrial soul, its heart is thoroughly medieval. Together with Krakow, Gdansk is a beautiful medieval city with brooding Gothic architecture and far fewer sightseers than the former. But, unlike Krakow, Gdansk suffered immense damage during the Second World War and what you see now is the result of decades of restoration.

Gdansk was founded in 997 and has changed hands frequently, between German, Russian and Prussian rule, during its lifetime, spending many years as an independent state. After the First World War it was designated a 'Free City', protected by the League of Nations but part of Poland. After the Second World War, Gdansk was gradually rebuilt and its shipyards became Poland's economic powerhouse. Poland's first post-Communist president, Lech Walesa, began his journey in the shipyards as the leader of Solidarity. Today the shipyards are idle, replaced by high-tech businesses.

A short bicycle ride up the coast is Sopot, where Poland's holidaymakers relax. It's a pleasant spa resort with Europe's longest pier and 5 kilometres (3 miles) of beaches. North of Sopot, the third of the Tri-City group, Gdynia, is a modern antidote to Gdansk's old-world charm: it has many examples of functionalist architecture and is worth a daytrip, but base yourself in Gdansk.

> "Together with Krakow, Gdansk is a beautiful **medieval** city with brooding Gothic **architecture** and far fewer sightseers than Krakow."

HOW TO GET THERE
Wizzair flies to Gdansk from Glasgow, Liverpool and London City airports. Ryanair also has a service to Gdansk from London Stansted.

CONTACTS/FURTHER INFORMATION
www.roppttk.pl
www.sopot.pl

St George Church, Sopot

068 KRAKOW

HOW TO GET THERE
easyJet, Ryanair, Jet2 and SkyEurope fly to Krakow from several UK airports.

CONTACTS/FURTHER INFORMATION
www.mcit.pl
www.kopalnia.pl
www.auschwitz.org.pl

Busy Krakow Square

Thanks to budget airlines and Poland's 2004 membership of the EU, the secret is out about Krakow. It has one of the most elegant and well preserved medieval city centres in Europe. Its Old Town is now a UNESCO World Heritage site, although that will not protect it from the avalanche of sightseers it now receives. However, during the Second World War, Krakow was protected from the devastation visited upon other Polish cities by the Nazis; perhaps because it was the headquarters of the governor installed by Germany.

The focal point of Krakow's weathered Old Town is the stately Rynek Glowny square, surrounded by Gothically-dressed buildings and spires including the city's old market hall, the grand Sukiennice. The square's adjoining cobbled streets, particularly Florianska and Grodzka, see the bulk of the action with bars, boutiques and restaurants. Polish cuisine has come a long way since its bleak Soviet years and many of the city's cellar restaurants serve good value meals, typically served with Polish beer. One treat is to spend the day seeking out tiny, hidden cafés and restaurants in the 15th-century side streets.

Wawel hill with its castle is a helpful landmark and south of Wawel is the Jewish quarter of Kazimierz where *Schindler's List* was filmed. The Museum of Jewish History explains what happened to Krakow's Jews during the Second World War. Many residents of Kazimierz were sent to Auschwitz-Birkenau concentration camp, the Nazi's largest concentration camp, 56 kilometres (35 miles) west of Krakow. You can visit the site from Krakow although it is not recommended as suitable for children under 14.

The Salt Mines

Eleven kilometres (seven miles) southeast of Krakow, the Wieliczka salt mines are an eye-opening experience. There are 322 kilometres (200 miles) of tunnels, but it's not the mine workings that fascinate but rather the underground salt sculptures and caverns formed into a glittering cathedral – even the chandeliers and statues of the Madonna are carved from salt. Thousands of local Poles worked in the mines, which are responsible for much of Krakow's wealth of architecture.

HOW TO GET THERE
LOT, Wizzair, BMI, British
Airways, Jet2, Ryanair and
easyJet fly to Warsaw from
many UK airports.

**CONTACTS/FURTHER
INFORMATION**
www.warsawtour.pl

Royal Park in Wilanow

WARSAW

Poland has benefited enormously from joining the EU in 2004 and Warsaw in particular is thriving. The centrally-located capital of this vast nation is its most cosmopolitan, modern metropolis although it remains approachable and friendly, just like its inhabitants. Poland's best nightlife, hotels and restaurants are here, ranging from grand cocktail-fuelled nights in the Column Bar of the landmark Le Royal Méridien Bristol hotel on the Royal Route to a hearty meal of Polish *pierogis* (dumplings) in a local restaurant where the welcome is as warm as the sour-rye soup on the hob. Bustling Nowy Siwat is the street where you'll find many of the city's drinking dens.

Warsaw, like most Polish cities except Krakow, was utterly destroyed during the Second World War; the Old Town was restored to its former glory, but most of the city's architecture dates from the 1950s onwards. Few cities have as tumultuous a history as the Polish capital and you can learn about Warsaw's recent past in the excellent Warsaw Uprising Museum, which opened in 2004. This is one of those cities that grabs your attention and refuses to let go.

Bialowieza National Park

Just over 161 kilometres (100 miles) northeast of Warsaw, this national park has the unusual distinction of being a UNESCO-sponsored Biosphere Reserve and World Heritage site. The reason? It's one of the few places in Europe where the original old-growth forest that covered the continent survives and it's a habitat for many of Europe's most endangered species. Much of Poland, outside of the cities, is a wild country and few places in Europe are as wild as the Bialowieza National Park. The park began life in 1541 as a royal hunting reserve – the quarry being the European bison, which has been reintroduced to the vast ancient forest. Other major mammals in the reserve include elk, wild boar and wolves – an on-site museum introduces the species. You can take wildlife-spotting tours or simply visit for a day, either way you won't find a greater contrast with the bright lights of Warsaw.

WROCLAW

HOW TO GET THERE
Ryanair fly to Wroclaw from
Glasgow, Leeds-Bradford,
Norwich and London Stansted
airports.

**CONTACTS/FURTHER
INFORMATION**
www.itwroclaw.pl

Handsome Wroclaw, to the west of Warsaw and close to the German border, is one of the stars of Eastern Europe. Thanks to its location, no other Polish city has as complicated a history as this. In the long run, however, Wroclaw has benefited from its outside influences to become arguably Poland's most cosmopolitan city.

With an Old Town reconstructed after wartime damage, and with dozens of bridges over the River Oder it resembles Prague, and thanks to the University of Wroclaw it also has a similarly lively night scene. Some beautiful examples of baroque architecture can be seen on the university campus but simply wandering around the Old Town will satisfy most sightseers; many of the sights, such as the cathedral and the medieval churches of Ostrów Tumski island are illuminated at night. A short circuit of the centre on foot, starting from Rynek, the city's broad market square, takes you past most of the sights. This leaves plenty of time for a beer in Piwnica Swidnicka, the city's most renowned cellar bar located below the 15th-century town hall on Rynek, before you end the day in the Pasaj Niepolda, the hub of Wroclaw's nightlife.

Zakopane and the Tatras

If it's good enough for a Pope, it's good enough for anyone. The Tatras, the highest mountain range in the Carpathian Mountains south of Wroclaw on the border with Slovakia, are where Pope John Paul II indulged his passion for skiing and hiking. They're an altogether more challenging proposition than the Alps, with only a basic infrastructure and a jagged landscape, but they have a special place in the heart of the Poles, being one of the few options for a holiday break during Poland's Communist years. Zakopane is the main resort in the Tatras and is just as busy in the summer hiking season from May to September as it is during the winter. You can drive to Zakopane from Wroclaw, although Krakow is closer.

Old Town

PORTUGAL

Portugal runs the length of Spain's western border, occupying most of the Iberian Peninsula's Atlantic coast. This coastline has been the source of much of Portugal's wealth, thanks to a strong tradition of sea-faring explorers and traders. The evidence of that wealth can be witnessed in the ornate architecture of the Portuguese capital Lisbon and the second city of Porto. The influences of centuries of trade and exploration to Africa, Asia and the Americas can be tasted in the national cuisine and heard in its music – visiting Portugal is a treat for all of the senses.

TIME DIFFERENCE GMT +0 (Western European Summer Time +1)

TELEPHONE CODE +351

CURRENCY Euro

LANGUAGE Portuguese

NATIONAL TRANSPORT WEBSITE www.cp.pt

POPULATION 10,600,000

SIZE OF COUNTRY 88,940 sq km (34,340 sq m)

CAPITAL Lisbon

WHEN TO GO The Algarve resorts of the southern coast are open almost all year round; winter sun can be hit and miss and the Atlantic beaches may be stormy, but the golf courses remain popular during these months. Portugal's cities are attractive throughout the year but are at their best during spring and autumn; spring sees Easter and Carnival celebrations too. Peak season, in July and August, can be uncomfortably hot.

TOURIST INFORMATION www.visitportugal.com

HOW TO GET THERE
easyJet fly to Lisbon's Portela airport from Luton, Monarch Airlines depart from London Gatwick. TAP Air Portugal also has frequent services to the city from London.

CONTACTS/FURTHER INFORMATION
www.visitlisboa.com

View From Esplanda Da Igreja Da Graca

LISBON

Via Brazil and North America, Portuguese explorers such as Vasco de Gama have set off from Lisbon to explore the world. It's hard to see what exactly compelled them to leave the Portuguese capital; this being such a beguiling and attractive city complemented in equal measure by modern projects such as the Metro and the city's dilapidated historic neighbourhoods. Like Portugal's melancholic fado music, Lisbon has a certain faded glamour. It clings to hillsides above the port; indeed the streets are so steep in places that a downhill mountain bike race takes place through the city's alleys every year. In 1755, on All Souls Day, an earthquake demolished much of the city and killed 40,000 people, many as they attended Mass. The city was rebuilt and the historic heart of Lisbon, the Baixa district, became what remains the grandest example of 18th-century architecture and town planning in Portugal. Based on a grid, straight wide streets lead to vast plazas, such as the main square, the Rossio. To the east of Baixa, the Castle of St George was the centrepiece of the city's defences since the Roman conquest of 138 BC. Centuries later the Moors constructed the Alcácova on the same hilltop site. Today the castle offers superb views over Lisbon.

West of the Baixa, Chiado and Bairro Alto are the most atmospheric quarters of old Lisbon. Smart department stores and chic boutiques line the narrow streets of Chiado. Parties erupt after midnight in the boisterous Bairro Alto where hole-in-the-wall bars open up to reveal artfully decorated interiors and a young crowd intent on knocking back caipirinhas and dancing to Latin-flavoured music. The Bairro Alto is also where you will find many of the city's fado houses – a visit to one is essential to any weekend in Lisbon. There are several excellent museums in the city centre, including the private art collection in the Museu Calouste Gulbenkian. Art lovers should also take a daytrip to the Cascais suburb of Lisbon, beyond the beaches of Estoril, where a new breed of contemporary art galleries is opening, attracting designer hotels.

PORTO

Portugal's second city has been designated a UNESCO World Heritage site and is a past European Capital of Culture. Accordingly, sightseers and culture vultures will be equally enthralled by the ancient city centre. Porto is more than 3,000 years old but it was when the port developed and trade between nations, including Britain, flourished in the 17th and 18th centuries that many of the city's most handsome buildings were commissioned. Today the city is much larger but the historic core can still be covered on foot comfortably and neighbourhoods such as the romantic Ribeira waterfront – a hotbed of trendy restaurants and bars – are practically inaccessible to cars.

Porto is a city of bridges and its highlights are found on the north side of the River Douro. Boat trips, in the flat-bottomed boats that once ferried wine barrels down the Douro are an exciting way of seeing the city from the water. The focal point of the old town is the cathedral, an imposing granite building close to the archbishop's palace. Shoppers should explore the streets that radiate out from the cathedral site. While the colourful, if shabby, streets of the old town are Porto's signature, the city also boasts some adventurous new architecture, in particular Rem Koolhaas's extraordinary, angular Casa de Musica, a concert hall on the edge of the old town.

HOW TO GET THERE
Ryanair fly to Porto from Bristol, Liverpool and London Stansted.

CONTACTS/FURTHER INFORMATION
www.portoturismo.pt

"Sightseers and culture vultures will be enthralled by the ancient city centre."

Boats on the River Douro

Port

Anyone with a passing interest in wine should make the short journey south of Porto, across the River Douro, to Vila Nova de Gaia, the home of the region's port trade. The rich, ruby-red fortified wine was particularly popular with the British, which is why so many of the wine lodges in the area have Anglo-centric names: Cockburn's and Graham's to name a couple. There are several varieties of port, from a light, white wine drunk as an aperitif to the heavier vintages uncorked after meals. But Portuguese wine growers are moving with the times and introducing more quaffable wines. Many of the wine lodges in Vila Nova de Gaia offer tours and tastings; the best is the tour at Sandemans on Largo Miguel Bombarda – it has a wine museum and great views of Porto.

ROMANIA

TIME DIFFERENCE GMT +2 (Eastern European Summer Time +3)

TELEPHONE CODE +40

CURRENCY Leu

LANGUAGE Romanian

NATIONAL TRANSPORT WEBSITE www.cfr.ro

POPULATION 21,500,000

SIZE OF COUNTRY 237,500 sq km (91,699 sq m)

CAPITAL Bucharest

WHEN TO GO Romania has extremes of temperature with profoundly cold winters and red-hot summers, making the spring and autumn months the best times of year to visit.

TOURIST INFORMATION
www.romaniatourism.com

Perhaps it was the years spent under Communist dictatorship or the country's low-profile accession to the EU in January 2007, but if any European country can be described as 'undiscovered' it is Romania. While the capital, Bucharest, has pockets of beauty among the vast, Soviet-inspired state buildings, the rest of this huge country is a bit of a slow starter. But that's fine, because among the miles of forest where wild boars and bears roam are, for example, some stunning castles. Journey as far to the east as Bucharest and you'll begin to realise what a vast and varied continent Europe really is.

BUCHAREST

In the city breakers' scramble to visit Eastern European cities after the fall of Communism and the rise of budget airlines, Bucharest was left behind by Riga, Tallinn, Prague and Ljubljana. But the capital of Romania, which entered the EU in January 2007, is catching up fast. Now, Bucharest is stepping out of the grim shadow of dictator Nicolae Ceausescu and returning as a more playful city. After all, Bucharest was known as 'Little Paris' in the 1900s, a playground of the East that was entertained night and day by theatre and music performed in the majestic Romanian Athenaeum music hall. Bucharest's golden age was the inter-war period when Europeans flocked to enjoy Bucharest's *laissez-faire* nightlife. The architecture of the city seemed to coordinate perfectly with this cultural high-water mark, with grand, baroque palaces such as the Cantacuzino Palace and delightful art-deco mansions – there's even a miniature Arc de Triomphe. Pleasure, for the Romanian aristocracy, was everything and they appreciated art without hesitation. You can get a taste of their high life at the National Art Museum and at the exuberant, art-nouveau museum of George Enescu, Romania's most famous composer.

Bucharest's planners also made space for numerous city parks, the most pleasant being Cismiglu Park, where locals play chess and watch tourists boating on the lake. Herastrau Lake, north of Piata Charles de Gaulle (yes, another French connection) is also worth a walk. Strolling along the boulevards of the old town and diving down the cobbled lanes of the Lipscani quarter are the best way to explore the city. You'll pass ornate churches glowing with gold-leaf alongside minimalist newly opened cafés and restaurants. But it is when the sun goes down that Bucharest reveals itself: from elegant soirées in the bar at the National Opera House to vodka-fuelled nights in backstreet bars, Bucharest is the perfect night-owl's haunt. It hasn't been transformed into a twee museum-piece just yet – which with so many reminders of the Communist era remaining, not least Nicolae Ceausescu's monolithic Palace of Parliament, this may prove difficult.

HOW TO GET THERE

British Airways flies to Bucharest from London Heathrow and Wizzair flies there from Luton. Austrian Airlines also have direct flights.

CONTACTS/FURTHER INFORMATION

www.romaniatourism.com

Financial Plaza

> "Bucharest was known as **'Little Paris'** in the 1900s, a **playground** of the East"

RUSSIA

TIME DIFFERENCE GMT +3 (Eastern European Summer Time +4)

TELEPHONE CODE +7

CURRENCY Rouble

LANGUAGE Russian

NATIONAL TRANSPORT WEBSITE www.rzd.ru

POPULATION 143,000,000

SIZE OF COUNTRY 17,075,400 sq km (6,592,849 sq m)

CAPITAL Moscow

WHEN TO GO St Petersburg has a surprisingly mild climate for a Russian city. Expect pleasant late spring and early autumn months but severe cold in the winter.

TOURIST INFORMATION www.visitrussia.org.uk

A global superpower, now retired, Russia spans Europe and Asia, bordering Estonia, Latvia and Finland on one side and China on the other. Cross the Bering Straits and you'll be in America. But it's the western end of Russia that we're interested in: the magical, monumental city of St Petersburg. From the Tsars to Stalin, the city bears the marks of all Russia's pivotal moments. On the one hand a glorious elegy to past monarchs, art and splendour, on the other it's a gritty, military port city where sailors stumble back to their ships after a night out. St Petersburg is anything but forgettable.

ST PETERSBURG

The former Russian capital, once known as Leningrad, is a city of impossible palaces, canals, technicolour churches and remarkable history. The city was founded by the Tsars in the 18th century using forced labour – Peter the Great gave the city his name until the Russian Revolution. Inspired by Venice and Amsterdam, Peter the Great carved great canals across the nascent city and commissioned vast, stately palaces.

Over the centuries the city has been a home to a pantheon of famous Russians, including Fyodor Dostoevsky and Aleksandr Pushkin, who called it a 'window to Europe'. It has survived some of the most brutal episodes in human history, including Hitler's 29-month siege of Leningrad when about one-third of the city's population of three million lost their lives. Still, though, it beats strongly as Russia's cultural and political heart – and compared to many European cities, St Petersburg still has the capacity to amaze and surprise.

Most people, of course, will have the city's palaces at the top of their to-do list. Europe's richest royal family, the Tsars, certainly left their mark on St Petersburg. Peter built himself a fortress that included a prison and cathedral while Catherine, his wife, preferred an elegant, gold-domed palace. Today, UNESCO recognises the city's historic heart with World Heritage status but there was no such protection during the Second World War when the Nazis used the antique furniture in the Catherine Palace as firewood. Catherine also commissioned the Hermitage – as a 'place of solitude' that only she could enter – and the Winter Palace. The absurdity of this is revealed when you realise the scale of the Hermitage: she could be alone here even with hundreds of people in the building. Now a world-class museum housing her extraordinary art collection – again, originally all for her appreciation only – the Hermitage contains three million artworks and makes for an unforgettable day out. Nights out are equally heady. The city's Kirov ballet boasts a role call of greats: Nijinsky, Nureyev and Anna Pavlova among many others. Just beware drunken sailors rolling back to their ships in the city's naval port.

> "Still, though, it beats strongly as Russia's **cultural** and **political** heart – and compared to many European cities, St Petersburg still has the capacity to **amaze** and **surprise**."

HOW TO GET THERE
Many national carriers, such as Lufthansa and Scandinavian Airlines, have flights from London to St Petersburg but you will have to make one stop. British Airways have direct flights from London Heathrow to St Petersburg's Pulkovo airport.

CONTACTS/FURTHER INFORMATION
www.petersburgcity.com

Orthodox Church

SLOVAKIA

TIME DIFFERENCE GMT +1 (Central European Summer Time +2)

TELEPHONE CODE +421

CURRENCY Slovak koruna

LANGUAGE Slovak

NATIONAL TRANSPORT WEBSITE
www.slovakrail.sk

POPULATION 5,400,000

SIZE OF COUNTRY 49,035 sq km (18,933 sq m)

CAPITAL Bratislava

WHEN TO GO Aside from the low-key ski season, there are few reasons for visiting outside the shoulder seasons of May–July and September. At these times, Slovakia is at its best. In July and August many Slovaks take their annual holiday, so accommodation does becomes harder to find.

TOURIST INFORMATION www.slovakiatourism.sk

The events of the 1990s, when Czechoslovakia broke apart, prove that Europe is in a constant state of flux. Slovakia is one of the offspring of its parent country and has grown into its new-found independence, joining the EU in 2004. Often confused with Slovenia, it lacks that country's zeal for tourism but still offers excellent outings in the mountainous countryside around the capital, Bratislava. Bratislava itself is a low-key city but it benefits from being outside the limelight. Slovakia is also well positioned between Austria and Poland to benefit economically.

BRATISLAVA

Property hunters and stag parties vie for seats on flights to the Slovak capital Bratislava, one of the youngest capitals in Europe. They're both in search of the same thing – low prices – and arguably both are missing the genuine charms of this tiny, historic city. With a population of just 450,000, Bratislava is never going to be a Central European powerhouse; its closest metropolitan neighbour is Vienna, just across the Austrian border. Like Vienna, Bratislava was part of the Habsburg Empire and retains much of the architecture of the period as well as a fondness for heavy stews and sweet cakes and pastries.

Bisected by the Danube, Bratislava's centre is divided between the handsome, medieval Old Town, punctuated by baroque palaces, and the socialist-era housing estates on the edge of town. Key sights include the city's castle, where you can climb the Crown tower for a superb view over the city to see the Old Town, the blocks of flats and the numerous bridges across the Danube. Many of Bratislava's churches are also worth a visit, especially the cathedral of St Martin, a monument to Gothic excess where up to 20 Hungarian kings and queens were crowned over 250 years of Habsburg rule. The pick of the palaces are the Primate's Palace, a baroque building close to the Main Square and site of many historic events, and the 18th-century Grassalkovich Palace, sometime venue of classical music concerts. The city has a packed programme of classical concerts, especially during the annual Summer of Culture (June to August) where music and shows are performed throughout the city.

Bratislava's tiny Old Town can be covered on foot in a matter of hours and one of the most popular ways of seeing the city is to meander from one bar to another sampling the local Kelt beer. Bratislava's nightlife has changed rapidly in recent years with the new wave of visitors encouraging stylish bars and clubs, although vast beer halls tend to mop up the rowdier element.

"Bratislava's tiny **Old Town** can be covered on foot in a matter of **hours**"

HOW TO GET THERE
Ryanair flies to Bratislava from London Stansted and seven other European airports including Bremen in Germany.

CONTACTS/FURTHER INFORMATION
www.bratislava.sk

Old Town alley

SLOVENIA

TIME DIFFERENCE GMT +1 (Central European Summer Time +2)

TELEPHONE CODE +386

CURRENCY Euro

LANGUAGE Slovene

NATIONAL TRANSPORT WEBSITE
www.slo-zeleznice.si

POPULATION 2,000,000

SIZE OF COUNTRY 20,257 sq km (7,819,sq m)

CAPITAL Ljubljana

WHEN TO GO With such a strong suit of outdoor activities, you'll want to time your visit to make the most of your activity of choice. Generally, unless you're enjoying the country's winter sports, this will mean May to October, with September considered the best month to visit. Alpine areas will be in bloom during April and May.

TOURIST INFORMATION www.slovenia.info

Perhaps one of the most dynamic economies in Europe, pint-sized Slovenia punches above its weight. This country is blessed with a sunny climate and a wealth of outdoor activities, from skiing to white-water rafting. Mountains, lakes and rivers are the venues for most of them, but the pretty capital Ljubljana exerts its own appeal. Slovenia is one of the countries formed from the break-up of Yugoslavia. While it has only a minuscule patch of coastline, on the Adriatic, it has quickly positioned itself as one of Europe's tourist hotspots. Get here now before it changes forever.

LJUBLJANA

Of all the cities opened up by the low-cost airline revolution of the 1990s, Ljubljana is one of the most engaging. Small enough to be explored on foot, Slovenia's bijou capital – a Prague in miniature – has been carefully preserved, although now the secret is out expect to see changes coming thick and fast. Like Bratislava, a river runs through the centre of Ljubljana. On the right bank of the Ljubljanica the Old Town encircles 15th-century Ljubljana Castle, set on a rocky promontory. From the castle's clock tower you can see beyond the grey suburbs to the forest hills that make up much of Slovenia. Picture-postcard pretty during the day, the cobbled streets of the Old Town come alive at night with bars and cafés and Ljubljana's young, cosmopolitan population. The baroque buildings of the Old Town are fast becoming homes to stylish boutiques so window-shoppers should set aside a morning for browsing on Stari trg and Gornji trg.

Art lovers won't feel left out either; Ljubljana has a strong art nouveau tradition, with the Dragon Bridge being one of the earliest examples. The Slovenian architect Joze Pecnik in particular left his mark on Ljubljana (as well as Vienna and Prague) between 1925 and 1944. He's the man responsible for all the classical columns in central Ljubljana. You can visit his house on the south side of the river. One building he can't take credit for is St Nicholas Cathedral and its gorgeous interior frescoes, illuminated by acres of gold gilt.

However, half of the appeal of Ljubljana lies in its proximity to Slovenia's rugged mountains, which are rapidly becoming the backdrop to a variety of adventure sports. To the north, the border with Austria is marked by the limestone Julian Alps where the intrepid can go white-water rafting on the Soca River or canyoning in its tributaries. The Kranjska Gora range has world-class skiing on a budget while the town of Bled wins plaudits for its idyllic lakeside location.

HOW TO GET THERE
easyJet fly to Ljubljana from London Stansted. The airport is 14 miles outside the city.

CONTACTS/FURTHER INFORMATION
www.ljubljana-tourism.si

Island in Lake Bled

SPAIN

TIME DIFFERENCE GMT +1 (Central European Summer Time +2)

TELEPHONE CODE +34

CURRENCY Euro

LANGUAGE Spanish

NATIONAL TRANSPORT WEBSITE www.renfe.es; www.metromadrid.es

POPULATION 44,700,000

SIZE OF COUNTRY 504,782 sq km (194,897 sq m)

CAPITAL Madrid

WHEN TO GO The beaches may be empty but many of Spain's resorts tick over in winter; Ibiza, for example, is a much trendier off-peak destination than during July and August. The south of the country has variable but mild weather during the winter, while the cities are interesting and enjoyable whatever the season: July and August are hot and busy and are best avoided.

TOURIST INFORMATION www.spain.info

Forget the Costas, there are far better things to do in Spain than bake on a beach. From Barcelona and Bilbao in the north – both vibrant, artistic cities – to the Moorish joys of Granada and Seville in the south, Spain's cities will entice anyone with an interest in art, culture or simply a chilled beer in a city square. What is most noticeable, however, is how distinct each city and region's character is. Barcelona is a wayward Catalan city while aristocratic, Andalucian Jerez has its own traditions of sherry and flamenco.

ASTURIAS

Known as the Costa Verde, the relatively unexplored region of Asturias occupies the northwest corner of Spain. It is blessed with 322 kilometres (200 miles) of coast, 100 undeveloped beaches and a mountainous landscape. But what makes Asturias extra special is that it is the hub of eco-friendly, green tourism in Spain. The contrast with the golf courses and high-rises of the Costa del Sol couldn't be greater than in the Picos de Europa National Park, Spain's most extensive protected area, at the northern end of Asturias. This is a wild world of tiny villages, Celtic traditions and one of the largest wolf populations in Europe, not to mention Europe's largest population of wild bears. If you don't fancy spotting the animals themselves, you can hunt prehistoric cave paintings of them instead. The Picos are just one section of the Cordillera Cantábrica, a mountain range running along the Asturias and into the Basque Pyrenees. It's undeveloped but far from basic.

If small, chic hotels are your thing, there are plenty of places to choose from – and they're increasingly likely to be sustainable projects using renewable energy and other environmentally friendly methods. The limestone gorges, oak forests and sheltered bays of the Asturias are also perfect to explore by bicycle or on foot; there's very little of the tourist traffic experienced in other parts of Spain. Even the local gastronomy is different: specialities include dairy produce and cider, bringing Asturias closer to Normandy or the West Country of England in taste. Similarly, you should bring waterproofs to Asturias since a high annual average rainfall is what keeps this land green and fertile. The rain doesn't deter the thousands of pilgrims who walk the Camino de Santiago along a variety of routes, all ending up in Santiago de Compostela, just outside the region.

Oviedo, the regional capital, remains a charming and cultured city with churches and a cathedral that repay investigation with world-class art and interiors.

HOW TO GET THERE

easyJet fly to Asturias from London Stansted; the airport is just west of Avilés in the centre of the region. An alternative is to take a ferry from the south coast of England to Bilbao or Santander.

CONTACTS/FURTHER INFORMATION

www.spain.info
www.asturiasinfo.com
www.oviedo.es

Lago de Covadonga, Picos de Europa

BARCELONA

HOW TO GET THERE
Low-cost airlines serving
Barcelona include easyJet,
Bmibaby and Jet 2. Iberia and
British Airways also have
regular flights to the city.

**CONTACTS/FURTHER
INFORMATION**
www.barcelonaturisme.com
www.spain.info

Geographically, Barcelona sits on the northeast coast of Spain. But culturally, the Catalan capital lies miles from the Spanish mainstream. Independent, radical, entrepreneurial and ever so slightly disdainful of the rest of Spain, they do things differently in Catalonia – the region even has its own flag and language as well as a thriving nationalism movement. Barcelona itself has long been an exciting and popular city break destination but there is much more to the city than Antoni Gaudí's admittedly out-of-this-world architecture and Las Ramblas.

Of all Spanish cities, Barcelona is the most outward looking and cosmopolitan. From backstreet bars and courtyard cafés to transsexual cabaret and avant-garde art galleries, Barcelona is a place to explore with your inhibitions set to minimum. A night that starts with a chilled fino in a tapas bar might progress to a seething flamenco club before culminating in a hip bar in the gritty Raval quarter. Nightlife is certainly

Catalan Cuisine

Forget the tired clichés of paella and tortilla; Catalan cuisine is in a league of its own. Barcelona is the birthplace of Spain's most celebrated chef, Ferrán Adria, the founder of El Bulli in Girona, north of Barcelona, a restaurant widely recognised as one of the very best in the world. For a new take on tapas, make a reservation at Comerç 24, on the street of the same name in Barcelona. The upmarket tapas bar is run by a protégé of Adria. But what makes Catalan cuisine so special? For the most part, it is the inventiveness and irreverence of Catalan chefs. The ingredients are familiar – Mediterranean vegetables, fresh fish – the combinations may not be. Dishes are typically small in size and punchy in flavour. And Barcelona's demanding diners keep even the best chefs on their toes.

Museu d'Art Contemporani

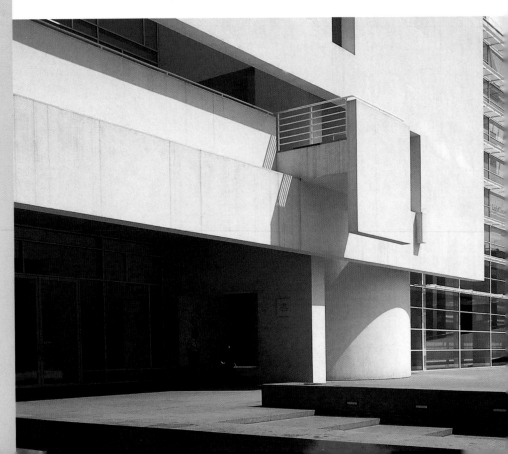

one of Barcelona's strengths so ensure you stay at a central hotel; it will make it easier to get back to your bed in the morning.

Barcelona is a large city – expansive enough to host the 1992 Olympics – but the main focus for most visitors is the Barrio Gotic (the Old Town), a tight knot of crowded streets around La Seu, Barcelona's distinctive Gothic cathedral. Running through the centre of the Old Town, Las Ramblas is the district's main street, through which most tourists run the gauntlet of street performers and pickpockets. While the Old Town is a victim of its own popularity, there are still must-see attractions here: the Museu Picasso and the Museu d'Art Contemporani. Once you've had a dose of modern art, escape the Old Town and head out to some of Barcelona's up-and-coming neighbourhoods. Northeast of the Old Town, the Olympic port and town is still somewhat sterile although there is a new crop of beach bars strung along the seafront from the port.

Casa Milà

Gaudí

Most people with a passing interest in architecture will have heard of Antoni Gaudí (1852–1926). The Catalan architect is responsible for some of the most spectacular buildings in Barcelona, including the Sagrada Familia, a basilica north of the Old Town district (so far north, it has its own Metro stop). The Sagrada Familia spotlights Gaudí's signature style: organic, surreal and never knowingly understated. Compulsively decorated with sculptures, spires and symbols, Gaudí spent 40 years working on his masterpiece and never completed it. Work is still ongoing and is expected to be completed some time in the 2020s. But even now, love or hate Gaudí's style, it's a remarkable sight.

HOW TO GET THERE
easyJet fly to Bilbao airport, which is 10 kilometres (6 miles) northwest of the city. Ryanair flies to Santander, a town several kilometres southwest of Bilbao. P&O's ferry service to Bilbao from Portsmouth departs every three days for most of the year.

CONTACTS/FURTHER INFORMATION
www.bilbao.net

Guggenheim Museum

BILBAO

Once a gritty, industrial port, Bilbao was transformed by Frank Gehry's dazzling Guggenheim Museum. The curvaceous, titanium-clad building soaks up attention but it isn't the only architectural wonder in the city: Norman Foster's underground metro stations use quirky glass tubes as entrances while the award-winning Euskalduna conference centre, more romantically known as the Euskalduna Palace, is an imposing design intended to resemble the last ship built in Bilbao's shipyards. To learn more about Bilbao's maritime tradition visit the Ría de Bilbao Maritime Museum in the old shipyards.

Work began on the Guggenheim Museum in 1991 and it opened its doors in 1997. The museum hosts frequently-changing exhibitions by Spanish and international artists as well as a permanent collection of modern art, including some gargantuan sculptures. But even giant, eye-catching works such as *Puppy* by Jeff Koons can be overshadowed by the magical building.

While the Guggenheim is clearly the flagship museum in the city, don't miss the Fine Arts Museum, close to the Guggenheim in Museo Plaza. It has one of the country's finest collections of Spanish art, spanning 800 years.

Eating in Bilbao

The sea suffuses Bilbao life: the cod-loving city is famous for its seafood but all food is taken seriously by the Basque locals, especially if it is regionally sourced. The rustic cuisine of the northwest has been refined but the powerful flavours of the food (anchovies, salt cod) and the wine (from the neighbouring provinces of Navarra and Rioja) continue. A great place to start your Basque quest is the restaurant at the Guggenheim, where Michelin-starred Basque chef Martín Berasategui is in charge of the kitchens.

GRANADA

Entering Granada's Albaicín neighbourhood is like walking through Alice's looking glass. The Andalucian city's ancient Moorish quarter, a small network of streets on the map, cascades down a hillside and, once you pass the 11th-century Arab Baths at the edge of the quarter, it seems to magically expand. Fortunately, it's no hardship getting lost in the Albaicín's lanes because each wrong turn yields wonderful views of Granada's other stand-out attraction, the Alhambra, across the gorge of the Río Darro. Both the Albaicín and the Alhambra are UNESCO World Heritage sites.

Just an hour's drive from the sweaty flesh of the Costa del Sol, Granada seems like a world away. To the southeast, the Sierra Nevada has Spain's highest mountain (Mulhacén) and Europe's most southerly ski station at Solynieve (sun and snow – although ski-able snow is patchy and fleeting). The southern side of the Sierra Nevada is known as Las Alpujarras (see panel) and is one of the most popular, year-round destinations for hikers in Spain. If you're here for a long weekend, two days in Granada and a day exploring Las Alpujarras would be enough time to see both.

Hiking in Las Alpujarras

The white-washed villages of Las Alpujarras are one of the most scenic spots in southern Spain. Among them is the highest settlement in Spain, Trevélez, where the high mountain air dries the region's delicious Serrano hams. Overlooking the Poqueira Gorge, at the western end of Las Alpujarras, the villages of Pampaneira and Bubión are popular bases for hikers and mountain bikers. There are some challenging walking routes in the shadow of Mulhacén, Spain's highest mountain with British tour operators and local firms offering guided walks. Pack sturdy boots and warm clothing because the weather can be unpredictable. As you travel east, on the A4132, the settlements get smaller and less touristy.

> "The **Alhambra** is an enchanting sight, easily the match of **historic** buildings in Rome or Athens."

First stop in Granada should be the Alhambra. Despite the convoluted entry requirements – its popularity means that you'll need to pre-book your tickets or be there as soon as it opens for the day – the Alhambra is an enchanting sight, easily the match of historic buildings in Rome or Athens. Expect to

HOW TO GET THERE
Ryanair fly to Granada from London Stansted, East Midlands and Liverpool. Granada is just a 90-minute drive from Malaga, served by most budget airlines and the national carrier Iberia (from London Heathrow).

CONTACTS/FURTHER INFORMATION
www.turgranada.es

The Alhambra

spend most of the day at the site. In the 11th century the Emirs of Córdoba (a city northwest of Granada) built a fort, the Alcazaba, on this hill. Over subsequent centuries, Moorish rulers expanded the fort until it featured four palaces and summer gardens. The 14th-century Casa Real is the heart of the complex, displaying the Moorish obsession with geometric architecture – often governed by the stars – and elaborate but delicate decoration. The soundtrack to viewing the exquisite Sala de los Abencerrajes and the Salón de Embajadores is that of trickling water. Look closely at the stuccoed panels and friezes and you'll see an Arabic inscription that reads, 'There is no conqueror but God'. In contrast, the original Alcazaba is a much more basic construction but from its tower there are superb views over Granada; it's easy to see why the Moors picked this spot for a fortress as they swept across Andalucia. The Moors controlled Granada and its

surrounding landscape from the 8th century until the 15th century when the Catholics gradually wrested southern Spain from them. But many of the cities of Andalucia, from Almería in the east to Seville via Córdoba and Granada retain extraordinary buildings and quarters built by the Moors.

Returning to the city centre is easy on the buses provided. A day out at the Alhambra should be followed with a meal in the city centre: Calle Navas and Calle Elvira, just behind Plaza Nueva, are two of the best streets for restaurants. On day two, explore the Albaicín, making your way up to the city's best viewpoint, the Mirador de San Nicolás (keep an eye on your possessions here). The Albaicín, also known as the Gypsy Quarter, is where numerous flamenco shows are staged, although their authenticity is very questionable. For real flamenco, go to Jerez or Seville (see pages 132 and 137).

Scenery in Las Alpujarras

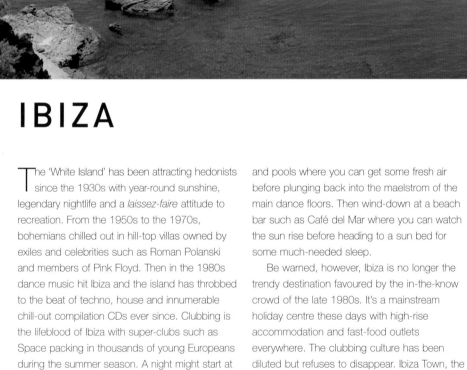

HOW TO GET THERE
easyJet fly to Ibiza from London while numerous ferry services connect Ibiza with mainland Spain at Valencia, Alicante, Barcelona and Denia.

CONTACTS/FURTHER INFORMATION
www.illesbalears.com
www.spain.info

Cala Xarraca

IBIZA

The 'White Island' has been attracting hedonists since the 1930s with year-round sunshine, legendary nightlife and a *laissez-faire* attitude to recreation. From the 1950s to the 1970s, bohemians chilled out in hill-top villas owned by exiles and celebrities such as Roman Polanski and members of Pink Floyd. Then in the 1980s dance music hit Ibiza and the island has throbbed to the beat of techno, house and innumerable chill-out compilation CDs ever since. Clubbing is the lifeblood of Ibiza with super-clubs such as Space packing in thousands of young Europeans during the summer season. A night might start at one of the countless bars in the West End of San Antonio, or in pre-club venues including Café Mambo which are popular for watching the sunset. The action then moves to the vast nightclubs outside the town: Privilege and Amnesia. The clubs have themed nights throughout the week, welcoming guest DJs from all over the world and entertaining clubbers with extravagant shows. Many have open-air terraces and pools where you can get some fresh air before plunging back into the maelstrom of the main dance floors. Then wind-down at a beach bar such as Café del Mar where you can watch the sun rise before heading to a sun bed for some much-needed sleep.

Be warned, however, Ibiza is no longer the trendy destination favoured by the in-the-know crowd of the late 1980s. It's a mainstream holiday centre these days with high-rise accommodation and fast-food outlets everywhere. The clubbing culture has been diluted but refuses to disappear. Ibiza Town, the capital, remains the chic corner of the island, the white-washed home of middle-aged bohemian expats, expensive restaurants, vintage shops and the island's most exclusive club, Pacha. The fashionable places to stay are the boutique hotels in restored fincas in the countryside, far away from San Antonio's teenage army. These tend to be in the north of the island, alongside secluded beaches and yoga retreats.

JEREZ

HOW TO GET THERE
Ryanair fly to Jerez from London Stansted. There are also frequent flights to the nearest large city, Seville.

CONTACTS/FURTHER INFORMATION
www.turismojerez.com
www.cadiz.es.

Cathedral, Cádiz

A night out in Jerez should begin with a small glass of chilled, pale, dry fino at one of the city centre tapas bars. Most people associate the Andalucían city of Jerez with sherry – as well as the performing horses of the Royal Andalucían School of Equestrian Art – and if a taste of some of the dozen, subtle variations can't challenge your opinion of the drink, nothing will. Try some of the more evocatively-named varieties, such as oloroso, amontillado and palo cortado rather than the sickly-sweet cream sherry popular in Britain. Jerez's sherry-producing bodegas, from the small family-run operations to heavyweights such as Gonzalez Byass and Harveys, offer tours and

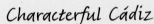

"And if you **overdo** it the night before, the aniseed-based **ánis** is a traditional, morning pick-me-up."

tasting sessions. They're located in and around Jerez's compact city centre. And if you overdo it the night before, the aniseed-based ánis is a traditional, morning pick-me-up.

Among Spaniards, residents of Jerez are renowned for their slightly superior attitude and expensive tastes; which might explain their interest in dancing horses. The displays of riding at the Royal Andalucían School of Equestrian Art on Avenida Duque de Abrantes amaze spectators.

Characterful Cádiz

Seedy but spell-binding, as only a port can be, Cádiz makes for a diverting daytrip from Jerez. The town is just an hour's train ride away on Spain's famously cheap national railway (www.renfe.es) and you'll arrive at the cruise ship terminal, on the edge of the old town. Cádiz is one of the great Mediterranean ports and was founded by Phoenicians. Money from the gold and silver trade built the city's gorgeous avenues and narrow streets of four or five storey houses and leafy plazas (tip: try the artisan ice cream at the hole-in-the-wall counter in the Plaza de Mina). However, that money has long since been spent and with the Med's fishing industry in trouble, Cádiz is becoming more faded by the day. In some ways, though, this adds to its appeal. The rock-bottom prices also attract a significant Euro backpacking community who also base themselves here to ride the waves at Tarifa, one of the top spots for kite and wind surfing in the world.

HOW TO GET THERE
National carriers, including British Airways and Iberia, fly to the Spanish capital from London Heathrow. Low-cost airlines Ryanair and easyJet also fly to Madrid from a greater range of airports around Britain.

FURTHER INFORMATION
www.esmadrid.com

Bar interior

MADRID

On the football pitch their teams are perennial arch-rivals; and Barcelona and Madrid are equally competitive city destinations. Where Barcelona is often cast as the popular and quirky rebel of the class, Madrid simply exudes style. The Spanish capital's inhabitants rival the Milanese in the fashion stakes, befitting a city that once counted David and Victoria Beckham among its residents. Dedicated followers of fashion should head for the streets of the Salamanca District, which are lined with big-name fashion boutiques. While Madrid fashion errs on the traditional side, there are exciting Spanish designers who, without the burden of expectation, push home-grown tastes into new areas. Salamanca's Calle Serrano, for example, spans the divide between the establishment, such as jeweller Carrera y Carrera, founded in 1885, and the contemporary, such as aristo designer Agatha Ruiz de la Prada who creates bold, colourful clothing for men and women. Victoria Beckham herself gave the

ultimate shopaholic's stamp of approval to Ekseption on Calle Velazquez, which stocks designer label clothes and accessories. In Calle Fuencarral punky little shops and stalls sell grungier designs for the more adventurous. Of course, for the traditional Spanish look you can buy finely-woven silk shawls or even matador outfits for men: bullfighting remains entrenched in Madrileno society, with the San Isidro festival in May signalling the start of the summer season.

The Spanish capital's appeal extends beyond exercising the credit card. Aside from the three world-class museums, lined up conveniently on Paseo del Prado (see panel overleaf), there are few pleasures greater than meandering from one spectacular plaza to the next. The most famous and perhaps the grandest of all is Puerta del Sol, just north of Plaza Mayor. The significance of Sol is far-reaching – all road distances in Spain are measured from this point so it is arguably the centre of the country. More relevantly, this is

Plaza Major windows

> "There's one **rule** to observe when going out for the night in Madrid; **don't** be **early**."

where the capital's main department stores are located, including the venerable El Corte Inglés. Sol and Plaza Mayor are touristy hubs and you won't want to spend too much time here, especially when there are stylish bars and restaurants to explore.

There's one rule to observe when going out for the night in Madrid: don't be early. Nothing gets going until the small hours, although revellers will warm up in tapas bars before midnight. Neighbourhoods like Las Letras are fertile hunting grounds for tapas lovers and there are numerous bars in the streets between Plaza Mayor and Paseo del Prado, such as Casa Alberto on Calle de las Huertas where Cervantes is thought to have written part of *Don Quixote*. As the clock ticks past midnight, men and women, young and old come out to play in what locals call the *marcha madrilena*. Venues come in and out of fashion so ask for advice from a local: there will be a venue for every taste from traditional flamenco haunts to glitzy nightclubs, gay or straight. Unstuffy but sophisticated, with a hedonistic streak, Madrid is a capital capable of pulling a few surprises on its visitors.

New architecture arrives in Madrid

In recent years the three largest museums in Madrid have had exciting extensions added. The costliest has been the £50 million addition to the Reina Sofia National Art Museum by Jean Nouvel, whose design adds a modern glass-fronted lift shaft to the exterior of the old building as well as a whole new, futuristic wing containing acres of space for the museum's collection of Miró, Dalí and Picasso (including the star attraction, Picasso's Guernica). The extension opened in 2005, making the Reina Sofia one of the world's largest contemporary art museums. If you arrived at the new Terminal 4 at Madrid's airport, however, your taste for contemporary architecture will have already been whetted by the beautiful, rippling roof. Madrid's Prado Museum received slightly less adventurous treatment from celebrated Spanish architect Rafael Moneo, befitting the museum's unrivalled collection of Spanish masterpieces from the 11th to 18th centuries, including Goya and Velázquez.

PALMA

Palma, the capital of Mallorca, is a small but intensely exciting Mediterranean city with outstanding food, shopping and sightseeing. Forget package holiday hell, Palma is a cultured and handsome gateway to Mallorca's unsung interior.

'Mallorca is poetry, light,' said Catalan artist Joan Miró, who lived on the island from 1956 until his death in 1983. If Mallorca is poetry, then its beautiful capital, Palma, the largest city in the Balearic Islands, is a perfectly crafted ode to art and architecture. Shaped by Romans, Moors and Catholicism, the city has buildings that are the match of any in Barcelona or Madrid. On the seafront, Palma's monumental gothic cathedral, La Seu, took 500 years to finish and was renovated

Tapas in Palma

The Mallorcan interpretation of tapas differs slightly from that of Andalucia, the home of tapas, but is no less enjoyable. Many of the dishes are simply miniaturised versions of main meals: tiny meatballs, finger-sized sausages and crunchy, fried whitebait. But there are some Mallorcan specialities, such as baby octopus fried in batter or *pa amb oli*, a staple snack of crusty bread rubbed with garlic and tomato and served with sea salt and olive oil. The restaurants La Bóveda and El Pilon serve some of the best tapas in Palma.

HOW TO GET THERE
easyJet has a daily service to Palma from Luton and London Gatwick airports. Flybe has flights to Palma from Exeter and Southampton three times a week. Ferries from Barcelona and Valencia to Palma take from five to ten hours to make the crossing.

CONTACTS/FURTHER INFORMATION
www.spain.info

Palma Cathedral

by Antoni Gaudí in the early 20th century. Next to the cathedral, the Palau de l'Almudaina is an ancient Arabic fort and part-time royal residence of King Juan Carlos of Spain. Visitors can tour the ornate State Rooms. And to the west of the city centre, beyond the Catalan Castell de Bellver, there is Miró's studio, now open to the public in the Fundació Joan Miró, itself a stunning modernist building.

But you don't have to dive into Palma's museums and art galleries immediately. One of the simplest pleasures of a weekend in the city is wandering the maze of alleys in the Old Town, a largely pedestrianised area just inland from the cathedral. Some of the mansions built by successful merchants from the 14th century onwards in this quarter are open to the public. Can Marques offers an intriguing glimpse into the lifestyle of Palma's elite but the most spectacular example is Palau March, the family home of one of the world's wealthiest men, Joan March. He spent his money on sculptures by Auguste Rodin, Henry Moore and Barbara Hepworth, all now displayed within sight of La Seu's buttresses.

Take time to explore the boutiques of the Old Town; shoe shops are a speciality but you'll also find branches of the Spanish department store El Corte Inglés and Zara. This all-year destination comes alive during the Christmas holiday season when the palm trees along the Passeig Marítim (sea front) are strung with lights and the shops stay open for longer. The old town can be covered on foot quite comfortably, although you should try to stay at one of the elegant town house hotels in the heart of the capital.

Palma is also a hotbed of new, design-led hotels. While some are a triumph of style over substance, a handful are true sybaritic retreats. For further seclusion, the craggy mountains of the Serra de Tramuntana are just a half-hour drive away and are sprinkled with luxury hideaways. A daytrip into the Tramuntana could take in Valldemossa, where Frédéric Chopin stayed, the orange tree-lined valley of Sóller and Lluc's monastery. Return to Palma for a final send-off in the city's excellent restaurants.

Mediterranean Balcony

HOW TO GET THERE
Flight options to Seville range
from the low-cost airline
Ryanair to British Airways and
Iberia from London airports.

FURTHER INFORMATION
www.turismosevilla.org
www.tablaoelarenal.com

Plaza de España

SEVILLE

Seville assaults the senses – but in a most enjoyable way. The citrusy scent of orange blossom, the plucking of a flamenco guitar, the Moorish architecture of Seville's Reales Alcázares: put them together and you have a magical weekend. What's more, this is a city dedicated to having a good time, as evidenced by the zeal with which Feria de Abril is celebrated. The Feria de Abril is as intoxicating an introduction to Andalucia as you are likely to encounter. This week of parades and parties, sherry tasting and flamenco dancing follows Semana Santa, which begins on Palm Sunday and will see hotels booked solid.

Sightseers are spoilt for choice with must-see sights including the Cathedral and the adjoining Giralda, a 12th-century minaret that survives from the Moorish conquest of the city. The Cathedral contains the tomb of Christopher Columbus who described the West Indies as having 'air soft as that in Seville in April'. The Giralda can be climbed; in fact, it can be climbed on horseback as it was designed with a spiral ramp. Even without a horse the views from the top are worth the effort.

Moorish Seville also survives at the Reales Alcázares, the Royal Palaces. These were built by the region's Moorish rulers but when power returned to the Christian kings of Spain they continued to add ornate extensions to the palace. In complete contrast to the splendour of the Alcázar, the old Jewish quarter of the city, the Barrio de Santa Cruz, is equally atmospheric with orange trees and tiny plazas at every turn.

Dancing the night away

Finally, Seville's marvellous flamenco heritage is illustrated in the Museo del Baile Flamenco, which opened in 2006. Flamenco is at the very heart of Seville and both are characterised by theatricality, musicality and passion. There are frequent workshops where you can have a go at flamenco, but if you simply want to watch a performance the best venues are *tablaos* (flamenco theatres) such as El Arenal. But what is flamenco? 'Flamenco is like our blues,' said jazz master Miles Davis. Each performance is an emotional lament or dramatic story framed in a series of set-piece songs and dances.

HOW TO GET THERE
easyJet and Ryanair fly to
Valencia from London
Stansted, Gatwick and Bristol.

**CONTACTS/FURTHER
INFORMATION**
www.turisvalencia.es

Arts and Science complex

VALENCIA

Poised to rival Barcelona for weekends away, Valencia is undergoing a period of rejuvenation. In 2000, Valencia's radiant, futuristic City of Arts and Sciences opened. The complex features a science park and planetarium and in 2005 its wonderful opera house, which bears comparison to the Sydney opera house, held its first full-length season. Architect Santiago Calatrava has applied a typically Catalan irreverence to the project and it has paid off; Valencia is bound to excite anyone interested in architecture and design. Things are also afoot down on the waterfront. Thanks to landlocked Switzerland, which as reigning champion had the right to choose the venue for its defence, Valencia hosted the 2007 America's Cup yacht race and prepared for the occasion with a makeover of the down-at-heel harbour area. New marina buildings, a sweeping breakwater and entertainment venues have all been constructed with an estimated price tag of 2 billion euros. With the new developments have come designer hotels, swish restaurants and smart terrace cafés.

But you don't have to be a salt-encrusted yachtie to enjoy Valencia. The city's Old Town, the meandering streets of the Barrio del Carmen, boasts a UNESCO-recognised Silk Exchange and Cathedral. This part of Valencia remains a down-to-earth place with gorgeous Gothic houses that are being restored. And anywhere that has a local drink – agua de Valencia – comprising freshly-squeezed orange juice and cava can't take itself too seriously.

Valencia, Spain's third city, was an important Roman base on the Mediterranean and takes its name from the Latin for 'vigor'. No longer a vital trading post, the city is busy building a new future for itself beyond the undeniable appeal of the Fallas festival in early March. The Fallas is famous for its parades of giant cardboard models seen careening down the city streets before, astonishingly, they are burned amid exploding fireworks. There are few fiestas quite like it.

SWEDEN

Sweden's cars may have a reputation for dullness, but the same could never be said of the country. Most of the major cities in this large but sparsely populated nation are in the south. The capital, Stockholm, ranks as one of the most beautiful cities in the world; strung across a series of islands, it's a sublime mix of ancient and modern where water becomes integral to the cityscape. The landscape around the capital has scope enough for adventure – island archipelagos, woodland and waterways abound and to venture north is to enter a wintry wonderland. Gothenburg and Malmö are equally appealing destinations.

TIME DIFFERENCE GMT +1 (Central European Summer Time +2)

TELEPHONE CODE +46

CURRENCY Swedish krona

LANGUAGE Swedish

NATIONAL TRANSPORT WEBSITE www.sj.se

POPULATION 9,000,000

SIZE OF COUNTRY 449,964 sq km (173,732 sq m)

CAPITAL Stockholm

WHEN TO GO The Swedish summer is short but sweet, with warm temperatures, lots of sunshine and long hours of daylight. Conversely, in some years the winters can be cold enough for the Stockholm archipelago to freeze over. This said, the Swedes know how to cope with winter and Stockholm itself can be a lot of fun over the Christmas period. Skiing in Sweden is limited to the northern reaches of the country, such as Äre, where daylight hours are short. Spring (late April to June) is an invigorating time of year.

TOURIST INFORMATION www.visitsweden.com

HOW TO GET THERE
Ryanair fly to Gothenburg from London Stansted. SAS have regular flights from London airports.

CONTACTS/FURTHER INFORMATION
www.goteborg.com
www.konstmuseumgoteborg.se

Winter sunset over Gothenburg

GOTHENBURG

Home to Scandinavia's largest university, Gothenburg is a cultured, lively city. Sitting on the southwest coast of southern Sweden, Gothenburg prospered as a fortified port. Swedes departed Gothenburg to see the world and immigrants arrived, which accounts for Gothenburg's un-Swedish cosmopolitan outlook. It is an open-minded, forward-looking place; it is not just the city trams that invite comparisons with San Francisco.

With 25 theatres and 17 museums, including the monumental Konstmuseum, the city's leading museum of art, Gothenburg is rich pickings for any culture vulture. The Konstmuseum is a good place to start; it's a good introduction to Scandinavian artists such as Edvard Munch, while also displaying Old Masters and modern work by the likes of Francis Bacon. But you'll have to move fast to fit everything in: the city's Maritime Museum is equally interesting and that still leaves 15 more museums.

Like Stockholm, Gothenburg is a watery city, surrounded by an archipelago of hundreds of islands. Broad waterways divide the city's neighbourhoods, which range from imposing, classically-inspired buildings to modern architecture. Again, a car is not required. Simply take one of the many boat tours of the city's canals or traverse the city on the vintage trams.

Most of the nightlife – from theatres to bars and restaurants – revolves around the Avenyn avenue. There are shops here too, but a more varied selection can be found in the Haga neighbourhood.

The city regularly punches above its weight in the Michelin Guides with a number of highly-rated restaurants, comparing favourably with Stockholm. And you don't need a Michelin-star budget to eat well; like Stockholm, the central market, the Stora Salluhallen, is a fantastic place to nibble on Swedish specialities from the food stalls.

Don't think that Gothenburg is just for foodies and theatre junkies: the city also boasts the largest and most popular theme park in Scandinavia, the Liseberg. Liseberg theme park opened in 1923 and it has a number of early rollercoasters and other classic attractions. The park's Christmas fair is a national event; at other times of the year Gothenburg has a superb line-up of festivals, covering everything from classical music to heavy metal.

KIRUNA

A weekend in the Arctic Circle isn't everyone's idea of fun, but Kiruna offers a couple of once-in-a-lifetime experiences. Before iron ore was mined in this industrial town it was an important place for the Sámi, the native Lapland people. You can learn more about their crafts and traditions in Kiruna's Samegarden museum or get a taste of the Sámi's largely reindeer-based diet in some of Kiruna's restaurants.

However, most people pitch up in Kiruna for two reasons: it is just 17 kilometres (10½ miles) from Jukkasjärvi, a village famous for the ice hotel built here every winter. And the winter also brings one of nature's most wonderful phenomena: the aurora borealis or Northern Lights.

Caused by solar particles colliding with the earth's atmosphere at the two poles, these kaleidoscopic streaks of light are unpredictable but magical. Most people will combine a stay at the Jukkasjärvi, Ice Hotel with winter sports, such as dog-sledding, in the surrounding arctic wilderness and hope that they are lucky enough to see the Northern Lights too.

Ice hotel

Every year since 1990, the designers of the original Ice Hotel count down the days until the River Torne freezes over. Then 10,000 tons of crystal-clear, metre-square chunks of ice are hewn from the frozen river and lugged onto land. It's a fresh start for the design of the Ice Hotel every year and every year it gets larger and more elaborate. Everything – from the glasses in the Absolut Ice Bar to the beds in the 100 rooms – is hand crafted from ice. Is it cold? Yes. That's why people stay only for a night or two. You'll need to wear a woolly hat in the bar and sleep on animal furs in the bedroom. But for a brief and extraordinary weekend, it takes some beating. There is a chapel, cinema and even a sauna. But timing is everything; the hotel melts in May.

HOW TO GET THERE
Direct flights from Heathrow on SAS from December to April. At other times a plane change in Stockholm is required, doubling the journey time.

CONTACTS/FURTHER INFORMATION
www.icehotel.com
www.discover-the-world.co.uk

Icehotel interior in Jukkasjärvi, Kiruna

STOCKHOLM

HOW TO GET THERE
SAS fly to Stockholm from several British airports, including London City, Edinburgh, Glasgow and Manchester. Stockholm's Arlanda airport is 42 kilometres (26 miles) outside the city but there are frequent train services into the city centre where you can pick up the T-bana (metro). Ryanair flies to two other airports, which are considerably further away.

CONTACTS/FURTHER INFORMATION
www.stockholmtown.com

Island in the Stockholm Archipelago

Swedes nickname their capital 'The Ice Queen' not just because of its austere elegance but perhaps also because in the winter the waterways between the 14 islands the city is strung over tend to freeze. But whatever the season, Stockholm, one of the most attractive capitals in Europe, makes for a sublime weekend away.

Breathtakingly beautiful, Stockholm is also breathtakingly cold in winter when many of its residents can skate to work along the frozen waterways. You can join them if you rent ice skates, a rucksack with a life line and a life jacket. Bring your own warm and waterproof clothes. This is the low season for tourism and while there are few hours of daylight, there is something very appealing about settling down with a mulled wine in one of the restaurants in Gamla Stan (the fairytale-pretty Old Town) or shopping at the Christmas fair where lanterns and glowing stars are hung between the stalls. Fittingly, for the city that brought the world 'Dancing Queen' (and 'Mamma Mia' and 'Waterloo' among other hits),

Stockholm's vibrant nightlife doesn't slow down in the winter either: the hip waterfront neighbourhood of Sodermalm to the south, with its maritime flavour, and stylish Stureplan to the north are packed with bars and clubs, as cool inside as the outside is chilly. An ABBA museum opened in 2008, worth a visit if your appetite for music isn't sated after dark.

While winter is an exciting and atmospheric time to visit Stockholm (just bring waterproofs), summer is when you truly get value for money. With daylight stretching almost throughout the whole day, you can't help but pack more into a weekend. Leave the ice skates at home because a bicycle – hired out across the city – is the perfect way of exploring Stockholm in the summer. With parks, waterfronts and flat traffic-free lanes, the city is a cyclist's dream.

Open-air art can found in the form of sculptures in the city's parks (try Millesgarden) but fans of modern art will want to get into the city's world-class galleries and museums such as the

outstanding Moderna Museet, which has one of the largest collections of modern art in Europe – and it's free to enter. Swedish design has also swept the world – in a very understated and efficient manner – and you can see some examples in the National Museum in Stockholm. The city itself is an architectural degree course encapsulated, with medieval gabled buildings in Gamla Stan, grand, *fin-de-siècle* houses and ultra-modern buildings in Sodermalm. Sodermalm is also the home of Stockholm's most exciting shops with international chains, such as H&M, and independent outlets competing for space.

Sweden is not as eye-wateringly expensive as it once was and prices for everything, apart from alcohol perhaps, are reasonable. Accommodation can be a bargain, with cheaper hotels and bed-and-breakfasts often immaculately clean.

Don't bother with an expensive rental car; public transport is excellent, including frequent ferries into the Stockholm archipelago (see panel); the island of Vaxholm is an hour away.

Stockholm reflected in the sea

Stockholm Archipelago

Stockholm's archipelago, where the sea, the sky and the rock merge together in shades of grey, is a remarkable and relaxing place. The archipelago consists of 25,000 islands reaching from Stockholm out into the Baltic. In the winter, budding blade runners can skate between the islands on the ice – you'll need to be very fit – but in summer you'll have to kayak, sail or take the easy option and use the local ferry services. Swedish tour operators, such as 30,000 Oar, run by Bengt Kull, offer tours of the archipelago. You can rent one of the thousands of beautiful cottages scattered around the islands or hop between the increasing numbers of luxurious boutique hotels. A good base for sea kayaking is the southerly island of Uto, where your only company on the water will be seals. Whatever you do in the archipelago, 'it's always an adventure,' says Bengt Kull.

SWITZERLAND

TIME DIFFERENCE GMT +1 (Central European Summer Time +2)

TELEPHONE CODE +41

CURRENCY Swiss franc

LANGUAGE German, French, Italian

NATIONAL TRANSPORT WEBSITE www.sbb.ch

POPULATION 7,500,000

SIZE OF COUNTRY 41,293 sq km (15,943 sq m)

CAPITAL Bern

WHEN TO GO Switzerland excels during both winter and summer. It appears to suffer no hindrances during the winter when, for example, trains run on time despite heavy snow. The Swiss mountain resorts are perfect for snow-sports holidays, but most are just as busy in the summer months with hikers and bikers. Many of the mountain resorts are open for summer visitors by July. In the cities, apart from the temperature, it may seem as if winter has barely any effect: just bring warm clothes.

TOURIST INFORMATION
www.myswitzerland.com

Until 1848 the separate cantons of Switzerland were regarded as independent states; even now, Switzerland – a paragon of neutrality – can feel like a patchwork of a country. Several languages are spoken and there is a non-committal attitude to the concept of Europe. But that doesn't stop the country running as if by clockwork. As one of the wealthiest nations on the continent, its cities are not short of options for *bon viveurs* and you can always burn off the calories on Switzerland's alpine mountainsides. While Swiss cities are clean, modern and safe, Swiss villages are clean, old-fashioned and ever so safe.

BASEL

Switzerland's second largest city is also the most industrialised, thanks to its port on the River Rhine and a burgeoning pharmaceutical industry that created, among other drugs, the first LSD. It has also produced the world's most successful tennis player in recent history, Roger Federer. But, still, it's an odd choice for a weekend away, unless you visit during Basel's two leading annual events: the Carnival in the winter and Art Basel in the summer.

Basel's Carnival comes in two parts: the Vogel Gryff festival at the end of January marks the banishment of winter, which is essentially an excuse to dance in the streets. Then on the Monday after Ash Wednesday, the Fasnacht spring carnival kicks into action at 4 am precisely. Parades of costumed revellers wind their way through the city and the bars stay open all night. Tuesday is children's day. On both days, extra trains are provided to ferry people to and from the party.

Art Basel is the world's largest contemporary art fair and has been described as the 'Olympics of art'. It takes place in June and typically features work from more than 3,000 galleries and 2,000 artists from 30 countries. While some deplore the commodification of art at fairs like this, the sheer variety, from sculpture and painting to video installations and digital art, will provoke sensory overload in others. The fair infects the whole of Basel with a fever for art; bars, restaurants, cafés and other venues join in the event. Children can get involved with special workshops and a kindergarten in the Art Kids programme, which is free. There are lectures, films and discussions about art for adults. While Art Basel will be of most interest to those working in the art world, for art lovers it's a chance to spot future stars before they hit the big time.

HOW TO GET THERE
British Airways, Swiss and easyJet fly to Basel from the UK.

CONTACTS/FURTHER INFORMATION
www.baseltourismus.ch
www.art.ch

The Old Town at winter

HOW TO GET THERE
Flybe flies to Bern from Birmingham and Southampton.

CONTACTS/FURTHER INFORMATION
www.berninfo.com

Ice Sculptures

BERN

It's the pub quiz question from hell. What is the capital of Switzerland? Are you sure it's Bern and not Zurich or Geneva? Yes, the Swiss capital is an unassuming, almost provincial town in the Swiss lowlands. Set on the River Aare, it seems to hug the contours of the river and the land; it's an idyllic setting and the Bernese know it, taking obsessive care in how tidy their city is. The name Bern derives from 'bear', the city's mascot since its foundation in 1191, but it wasn't until 1848 that Bern was elected capital of Switzerland. The bear associations still hold: one of Bern's most popular tourist attractions is its bear pit, the *barengraben*, where the resident bears look exceptionally well-fed and are treated like royalty.

Bern's other main area of interest is the Old Town, a UNESCO World Heritage site that sticks out into the River Aare. Towering above the Old Town is the spire of its Gothic cathedral, the tallest spire in Switzerland. Walking away from the river, you'll encounter the Bundeshauser, the Swiss parliament, which you can tour. For such a small city, Bern has more than its fair share of museums, with pride of place going to the Paul Klee Centre, which boasts the largest collection of the artist's work, and the Museum of Fine Arts' collection of Italian masters.

A one-time resident of Bern, Albert Einstein, used his time working in the stultifying dull patent office to come up with the General Theory of Relativity in 1905. You can test his understanding of gravity at two ski resorts within a two-hour train journey of Bern; Grindelwald and Wengen. The Bernese Oberland is also very close and well known for its cross-country skiing routes, snow permitting.

Lucerne Daytrip

The city of Lucerne is on the western shore of Lake Lucerne, the closest side to Bern, which is to the west and just over an hour away by train. Lucerne is the centre of Switzerland's lakeland, surrounded by scenic and rugged mountains. Lucerne, the largest of the lakes, can be toured by paddle steamer. Many of the smaller lakes have myths and legends attached to them, such as the story of William Tell, which is set on Lake Uri.

GENEVA

Geneva is out on a limb, surrounded in the very western corner of Switzerland by the French Alps. It's an international city with more than 250 international organisations resident here, such as the World Health Organisation. But this doesn't detract from the very Swissness of the city: it's clean, affluent, safe and comfortable. And the trains run on time, which is great news for anyone heading onward to the superlative alpine winter resorts. Zermatt is three hours away and the home of alpinism, Chamonix, is just over an hour away. Mountain sports – summer or winter – are the primary reason people pass through Geneva. It has good restaurants, some interesting museums and a large lake, but the fact is that most people will be checking timetables for the train out.

Geneva's great blessing is its proximity to Chamonix. The French mountain town is the alpha alpine town. Whether you're into skiing, snowboarding or ice climbing in the winter or mountain biking, canyoning and paragliding in the summer, Chamonix is the place to get an adrenalin fix. It's not the cheapest, or the steepest (that would be La Grave), but with 2,743 metres (9,000 feet) of descent and Mont Blanc in the windshield, who's complaining? The world's oldest mountain guide organisation, La Compagnie des Guides de Chamonix, was founded here in 1821 and since then the town has been the front room of the European climbing fraternity. Tourism and extreme sports are the town's *raison d'être* and you'll need nerves of steel to attempt some of the off-piste ski runs and climbing routes here. The Aiguille du Midi cable car is particularly nerve-wracking for those without a head for heights. The two resorts of Chamonix and Zermatt are linked by the Haute Route, a famous ski touring route across the mountains first ploughed by British mountaineers in 1861. The route hits 3,658 metres (12,000 feet) in altitude and can be completed in seven days, weather permitting. In summer these mountains are a playground for mountain bikers.

HOW TO GET THERE
BMI, Flybe and Swiss all fly to Geneva from UK airports. easyJet has the widest coverage, departing from Belfast, Bristol, Edinburgh, Liverpool, London Gatwick, Luton and Stansted, Newcastle and Nottingham for Geneva.

CONTACTS/FURTHER INFORMATION
www.geneve-tourism.ch
www.chamonix.com

The Matterhorn

ZURICH

HOW TO GET THERE
Swiss, BMI and British Airways fly to Zurich from UK airports. The high-speed TGV rail link from Paris takes about four and a half hours.

CONTACTS/FURTHER INFORMATION
www.zuerich.ch
www.kunsthaus.ch
www.zermatt.ch

Street party

On the surface, Zurich might appear to be a city of well-fed bankers and black Mercedes limousines. But underneath that popular perception an increasingly hip city is struggling to get out. For all the stuffy convention that Switzerland's wealthiest city displays, it might surprise you to learn that this was the home of the absurdist Dada art movement and the art 'happening' Cabaret Voltaire. Even in 2005, the summer's art season was marked by the installation of hundreds of 1.5-metre (5-foot) teddy bears around the city.

The Swiss ski resort of Zermatt – overshadowed by the Matterhorn, a mountain that resembles nothing so much as a chunk of Toblerone – is five hours by train from Zurich. But while some Swiss cities are solely regarded as wintry gateways to Alpine ski resorts, Zurich is at its best during the summer. The water of Lake Zurich, fed by the River Limmat, is so clean as to be drinkable. There are water sports and swimming spots all along the lake and the river and you can cool off at 18 beaches in the heart of the city, many of which convert to open-air lounge bars at sundown. Boat trips and bike rides around the lake are also popular, with bicycles freely available (with a deposit) from the central train station and myriad signposted cycle paths out of the city.

Zurich has two stand-out churches – Grossmunster and Fraumunster – the latter has stained glass windows by Marc Chagall. The Kunsthaus museum (the Museum of Fine Arts) holds the largest collection of works by Swiss and foreign artists in the country, including some fine Impressionists and Dadaists.

Most surprising is Zurich's rejuvenated nightlife. The hippest bars, clubs, restaurants and boutiques are found around Langstrasse in the post-industrial area of Zurich West, north of the train station. The Seefeld neighbourhood remains a good spot for socialising.

TURKEY

Currently engaged in negotiations to apply for EU membership, it seems Turkey has decided which way to swing. At the crossroads of Europe and the Middle East, Turkey has complex political and religious imperatives. However, that doesn't stop Istanbul being one of the liveliest and engaging cities on the Mediterranean. Wearing its Eastern influences proudly – after all, the city was the end of the Silk Road – Istanbul is an exotic and enticing place to spend a weekend. If there's time, combine it with a visit to the Turquoise Coast, every bit as lovely as the name suggests.

TIME DIFFERENCE GMT +2 (East European Summer Time +3)

TELEPHONE CODE +90

CURRENCY Turkish lira

LANGUAGE Turkish

NATIONAL TRANSPORT WEBSITE www.tcdd.gov.tr

POPULATION 74,000,000

SIZE OF COUNTRY 779,452 sq km (300,948 sq m)

CAPITAL Ankara

WHEN TO GO Istanbul is best visited during spring and autumn (April, May, June and September to October); it's hot and hectic in mid-summer. With a Mediterranean climate, winters here can be wet and variable.

TOURIST INFORMATION www.tourismturkey.org

094

HOW TO GET THERE

British Airways, Turkish Airlines and easyJet fly to Istanbul from UK airports. British passport holders will require a visa, which can be bought on arrival.

CONTACTS/FURTHER INFORMATION

www.istanbul.com

Sunset over the Blue Mosque

ISTANBUL

East doesn't so much collide with west in Istanbul as sit down for an animated chat over a hookah pipe in a street side nargile café. Since Istanbul joined the budget airline circuit in 2006 when easyJet inaugurated its Luton to Istanbul service, the Turkish city has gone to the top of the list for an exotic weekend break, although it has been a hip choice for the cognoscenti for far longer than that.

The Bosphorus divides Europe from Asia and western Istanbul from the Asian eastern side of the city – the two halves are linked by the Galata bridge. The two districts in which you will spend most of your time are the Sultanahmet Peninsula, where the city was founded on the Bosphorus, and Beyoglu on the other side of the Galata bridge. The best way to appreciate Istanbul is to let your senses lead the way. The Istanbul skyline is incredibly beautiful with minarets from the city's mosques framed against Ottoman palaces and hazy summer skies. Non-Muslims can visit Istanbul's Blue Mosque in Sultanahmet outside prayer times. The Aya Sofia, next to the Blue Mosque, is where Christianity and Islam meet in a 6th-century building that was the world's largest cathedral for a millennium. Two thousand years of history permeate every inch of Istanbul, which has been part of Ottoman and Byzantine empires, brought together in the Topkapi Palace.

While Istanbul's sights are extraordinary, the city offers the full package to weekenders. Many of the city's palaces have been converted to chic boutique hotels while cocktail bars and nightclubs add to Istanbul's 24-hour social scene. There are plenty of kebab shops and there are also many superb restaurants set in gorgeous locations from ancient rooftops to buzzing waterfronts. The Grand Bazaar is worth a visit for the sensory thrill but don't expect any bargains. Then relax in one of Istanbul's steamy hammams.

With Turkey campaigning to join the EU, travel to Istanbul couldn't be easier. The city will be a European Capital of Culture in 2010 so Istanbul will only get better as a short break destination.

UNITED KINGDOM

Comprising England, Wales, Northern Ireland and Scotland, the United Kingdom is a mongrel nation. As an island it has always nipped at the heels of continental Europe, sometimes unwilling to get too involved but not wishing to be left out. England's capital city, London, is one of the world's great centres, a crossroads of money, people and ideas. The devolved capitals of Cardiff, Edinburgh and Belfast have similarly intriguing histories. Britain's regional cities can always provide a weekend's entertainment, although thanks to a comprehensive if slightly threadbare transport network, it's not difficult to get away from the city centres and into the countryside.

TIME DIFFERENCE GMT +0 (British Summer Time +1)

TELEPHONE CODE +44

CURRENCY Pound sterling

NATIONAL TRANSPORT WEBSITES www.nationalrail.co.uk; www.tfl.gov.uk

POPULATION 60,000,000

SIZE OF COUNTRY 244,082 sq km (94,241 sq m)

CAPITAL London

WHEN TO GO The British weather is notoriously fickle, thanks to a maritime climate. With rain possible on any day, somewhere in the country, the best idea is to take your chances. Highland areas of Scotland can be very exposed in the winter but the rest of the country may only have a week or two of snowy weather from November to March. Summers can be very hot or very wet. London, to the east, is drier than average while Wales and the West Country tend to receive the bulk of the rainfall.

TOURIST INFORMATION www.visitbritain.com

095

BELFAST

HOW TO GET THERE

easyJet and Jet2 fly to Belfast from mainland airports. Stena Line ferry services cross the Irish Sea from Stranraer in Scotland to Belfast.

CONTACTS/FURTHER INFORMATION

www.gotobelfast.com

Bigfish sculpture

After decades of uncertainty and appearances on news bulletins for all the wrong reasons, Belfast is finally reaping the reward of devolution and the return of the Northern Ireland Assembly to the Stormont Parliament building in 2007. Visitors are flocking to the city, many seeing Belfast's attractions for the first time. The city has responded to the boom with new hotels, bars and restaurants opening all the time, adding a layer of luxury to what has been a famously gritty place.

While the dark days of the 1970s in the capital of Northern Ireland seem a long time ago, many visitors seek out evidence of the Troubles. One of the most popular sightseeing trips uses black cabs to take visitors to the epicentre of Belfast's sectarian strife, the Falls Road and Shankill Road to the west of the city. Here, the vast murals painted by Loyalist or Republican sympathisers will be explained by the taxi driver. The heavily fenced Peace Line between the Catholic and Protestant communities is also part of the tour. It's an educational and disturbing experience.

Thankfully, Belfast has much more to offer than a dark history. The Harland and Wolff shipyard is where the Titanic was built and the Ulster Folk and Transport Museum has an exhibition dedicated to the doomed liner.

The area around Belfast's Queen's University is where many of the city's museums and galleries (also the excellent Botanic Gardens) are located and this is a good place to spend an evening; an alternative is the optimistically-named Golden Mile.

The very stately Stormont building is set inside parkland; you can visit the park and see the outside of the building during the day but for a tour of the interior you'll have to be sponsored by an Assembly member. It's a sobering thought to recall how much hope has been invested in this building.

The Giant's Causeway in County Antrim, a remarkable shoreline of 40,000 basalt columns produced by volcanic explosions, is Northern Ireland's only World Heritage site and it can be reached on a daytrip from Belfast. You might like to make it a more leisurely visit and tour the nearby Bushmills Irish whiskey distillery too.

" Visitors are **flocking** to the city, many seeing Belfast's **attractions** for the first time. "

CARDIFF

Past and present collide in the Welsh capital. The city has several outstanding historic sights, including Cardiff Castle, a Norman fortress dating from Roman times that underwent extravagant interior redecoration at the hands of the third Marquess of Bute – at one time the richest man in the world – and his eccentric designer William Burges in the 19th century. Recent redevelopment has also improved many parts of Cardiff, in particular the docks (re-branded as Cardiff Bay) where coal mined from the valleys north of the city made its way out of Wales. Today, swish restaurants sit next to designer hotels such as the opulent St David's Hotel and Spa. Investment has also been made in state-of-the-art attractions such as the family-friendly, interactive science centre Techniquest and the Wales Millennium Centre. This superb multi-purpose arts centre is an attractive venue for every sort of show from musicals and theatre to stand-up comedy and opera. Mainstream or alternative, it's all welcome at the Millennium Centre.

With constructions like the Millennium Centre in the docks, new architecture in Wales is on something of a high. The country, like Scotland, has its own regional government, the National Assembly for Wales, which is devolved from London's Parliament. However, unlike Scotland's parliament building, the highly energy-efficient Welsh Senate building, also in Cardiff Bay, is widely regarded as an architectural triumph. It was designed by Richard Rogers and was intended to be as 'green' a building as possible, combining traditional Welsh materials and new technology. Costing £67 million, it was over budget but a fraction of the cost of the Scottish Parliament. Even if you're short on time, you should have a look inside.

Cardiff's repertoire of entertainment is also in a different league these days. It boasts one of the best sports and concert stadiums in Europe, in the futuristic shape of the Millennium Stadium.

> "Cardiff's repertoire of **entertainment** is also in a different league these days. It boasts one of the best **sports** and concert stadiums in **Europe**"

HOW TO GET THERE

There are direct train services from many UK cities, including London and Manchester. By road, take junctions 29 or 30 off the M4. Several airlines fly to Cardiff's airport, including BMI, Thomsonfly and Flybe.

CONTACTS/FURTHER INFORMATION

www.visitcardiff.com

Millennium Centre

097

HOW TO GET THERE

The Caledonian Sleeper is an overnight train service from London to Scotland run by First ScotRail and stopping at Edinburgh. Other train operators stopping at Edinburgh Waverley station are GNER and Virgin Trains. easyJet fly to Edinburgh from Belfast, Bristol, London Luton, Stansted and Gatwick.

CONTACTS/FURTHER INFORMATION

www.visitscotland.com
www.adventurescotland.com
www.7stanes.gov.uk
www.thehubintheforest.co.uk

Scott Memorial, Carlton Hill

EDINBURGH

Edinburgh, the Scottish capital, is one of the world's great cities. Not for its scale – its centre is compact and easily navigated on foot – but for its depth. The city has had royal connections since the 12th century, although Scotland has a particularly turbulent history. Edinburgh Castle is at the centre of a spell-binding skyline, especially when viewed from the summit of Calton Hill. Edinburgh was settled over a range of hills and the first inhabitants settled on the top of the castle's rocky promontory in the Bronze Age. By the Middle Ages, it was the home of Scotland's monarchs, until the union with the rest of Britain in 1707. Those monarchs would have been crowned on the Stone of Destiny, now displayed at the castle since its return from London in 1996.

While the Scottish monarchy is no more, the country has gradually acquired more political independence from London and the new Parliament buildings are a short walk from the castle at the end of the Royal Mile. Next to them, in Holyrood Park, is the Palace of Holyroodhouse, the Queen's official residence in Scotland. You can tour the state rooms daily. The streets coming off the Royal Mile are filled with boutiques, pubs and bars and some surviving medieval buildings. There's lively nightlife in this area but for a slightly hipper Edinburgh experience make the trip across the city, through the Georgian squares of the New Town to Leith. Don't be put off by its gritty representation in Irvine Welsh's *Trainspotting*: this waterfront quarter is where the city's best restaurants are located.

Edinburgh Festival

The Edinburgh Festival, including its Fringe, is the world's largest arts festival, taking over the city for the month of August. Every venue with space for a stage, however tiny, and at least a couple of seats for an audience, is pressed into service. It's a manic time to visit Edinburgh and accommodation is booked months in advance. Sightseers would do well to see Edinburgh at another time, but if you want to find yourself laughing helplessly at an obscure comedian in the back room of a pub, this is the occasion.

Adventure in Edinburgh

You don't have to go all the way to the Scottish Highlands to find adventure; in Edinburgh the great outdoors is on your doorstep. It's very easy to get out of the city centre for a day of climbing, horse riding or mountain biking. The 7Stanes (Scottish for stones) is a necklace of seven purpose-built mountain biking centers, strung east to west across the Scottish Borders. From Kirroughtree, overlooking the Irish Sea, to Glentress, a 40-minute drive south of Edinburgh, the 7Stanes have earned a worldwide reputation for high quality, man-made, all-weather trails, graded for difficulty, like ski runs, from green to blue to red to black. Glentress is the largest and most popular, not least because of the Hub Café and shop/bike rental run by former pro racers Emma Guy and Tracy Brunger. There are trails for all abilities, all offering stunning views over the Pentland hills. Also in those hills are several horse-riding centres offering pony trekking on hardy Icelandic ponies. You can take lessons or join organised rides in the low-lying Pentlands. But if you have a head for heights, there's only one place to go: the world's largest indoor climbing centre, which is in Ratho, close to Edinburgh's airport on the west of the city. Whatever the weather, you can test your skills in the stunning surroundings of the Edinburgh International Climbing Arena. The centre, which includes a spa and gym, is built into the walls of a quarry and natural stone cliffs alternate with artificial climbing walls. It's an outstanding facility and a great place to pick up some tips before venturing into Scotland's real mountains.

Linlithgow Palace

098

GLASGOW

HOW TO GET THERE

The Caledonian Sleeper is an overnight train service from London to Scotland run by First ScotRail and stopping at Glasgow. easyJet fly to Glasgow from Belfast and Bristol plus London Luton, Stansted and Gatwick.

CONTACTS/FURTHER INFORMATION

www.visitscotland.com
www.seeglasgow.com

SECC building

Glasgow, the gritty, ship-building city, might have a forbidding reputation but for art lovers there are few more exciting or rewarding cities in Britain or Europe. In many ways, Scotland's second city and the almost impenetrable dialect of its citizens are everything its capital, Edinburgh, isn't: post-industrial, with an eye for originality and bold architecture, as opposed to stately Edinburgh with its lawyers, bankers and politicians. From radical modern architecture to graceful 19th-century houses, there's plenty to see in Glasgow.

Glasgow's artistic connections go all the way back to the Glaswegian architect Charles Rennie Mackintosh. It was Mackintosh who infused conventional art nouveau with the naturalistic simplicity of the arts and crafts movement. His masterpiece is now the Glasgow School of Art at 167 Renfrew Street. A student at the school, in 1896 Mackintosh won a competition to design its new premises and he never looked back. The Mackintosh Trail guides sightseers past many of his designs. Mackintosh wasn't the only Glaswegian with a passion for beauty. Sir William Burrell was born in the city in 1861 and made his fortune as a shipping magnate. With enormous wealth at his fingertips he amassed a vast and eclectic collection of art which he bequeathed to the city in 1944. Burrell was a magpie with superb taste, buying Rodin sculptures, Degas paintings, rare tapestries, Ancient Greek pottery and Oriental carpets and all are on display in The Burrell Collection, Pollock Park. The Hunterian Museum in the University of Glasgow is a similarly enthralling museum with a collection spanning art and science. It was dedicated to the city by Dr William Hunter, a former student of the university, and it contains more than a million items (not all of which are on display).

Glasgow's family-friendly Science Museum should be added to your itinerary too. But the final showstopper is the newly restored Kelvingrove Art Gallery and Museum, Scotland's most-visited attraction.

HOW TO GET THERE
London has four major airports, Heathrow, Gatwick, Stansted and City, with flights from most international airlines arriving at least one of them. Luton airport is also a short train journey from central London. The major train stations in London are King's Cross, St. Pancras, which is also the Eurostar terminal, Liverpool Street, Waterloo and Euston.

CONTACTS/FURTHER INFORMATION
www.visitlondon.com
www.english-heritage.org.uk
www.nationaltrust.org.uk
www.tfl.gov.uk

Big Ben at night

LONDON

The one thing you might wish for more of during a weekend in London is time. Otherwise, the city has got pretty much everything else covered. World-class museums and galleries? Check. Iconic buildings, old and new? Check. Eateries for every budget? Check. It's impossible to cover all of London, Europe's most diverse and influential capital city, in a single weekend. Luckily, it's easy to get around the areas of interest using public transport, so you can range widely across this enthralling city.

The River Thames divides north from south London so a boat trip along the Thames will give first-time visitors a good sense of the city's geography. Many of the city's leading sights are north of the river – the major shopping areas of Covent Garden and Knightsbridge, the museums of South Kensington and the bars and gastro-pubs of Clerkenwell – but the South Bank opposite the Houses of Parliament has some of the capital's most interesting attractions: Shakespeare's Globe theatre, the London Eye, the Tate Modern gallery and the performance venues of the Royal Festival Hall.

Crossing the Millennium Bridge from the Tate Modern building, a gigantic converted power station, takes you towards St. Paul's cathedral, which celebrated its 300th anniversary in 2008.

London's Parklife

It can be a surprise to find that London has an abundance of green, sometimes wild, spaces. London's Royal Parks include Hyde Park, St James's Park near Buckingham Palace and Regent's Park where London Zoo occupies a corner. As you get further from the centre, the less manicured the parks get. Richmond Park, London's largest Royal Park, has a herd of 650 deer, while Hampstead Heath in north London has many wildlife-watching opportunities including bat-spotting walks in the summer months. Summer is when London's parks are at their best and busiest with cyclists, roller-bladers and sunbathers. To cool off you can take boat trips on the Serpentine in Hyde Park or swim in the pools of Hampstead Heath.

Dancers at the Notting Hill Carnival

" ... the city comes **alive** for visitors when it **reveals** its less **well-known** corners ... "

The cathedral's dome, the only one in Britain, is second in size only to St Peter's in Rome and was the work of Sir Christopher Wren. Climb the 530 steps to the Golden Gallery for superb views across the capital. This part of northeast London, including Clerkenwell, Spitalfields, Shoreditch and Brick Lane, is an exciting place to go out at night, with thriving restaurants, pubs and bars. The area is also rich in history: Charles Dickens set some of his novels in the Inns of Court and east London, and for real-life intrigue you can also follow in the footsteps of Jack the Ripper.

Start the next morning with breakfast in central London – Marylebone has some excellent cafés – before setting off for the day. Shoppers will be on the doorstep of the biggest names in shopping: Selfridges on Oxford Street, the boutiques of New Bond Street and the King's Road and Harvey Nichols and Harrods in Knightsbridge. South Knightsbridge is home to three of the best museums in Europe; the Natural History Museum, the Victoria & Albert Museum and the Science Museum – all with free entry.

While many of London's features are recognised all over the world – from London Bridge to Buckingham Palace – the city comes alive for visitors when it reveals its less well-known corners: the havens of tranquillity such as Chelsea Physic Garden or Little Venice's canals, or the Georgian village of Hampstead and its celebrity residents past and present.

London Daytrips

Even hardened Londoners like to get out of town now and then. Two of the favourite daytrips, both to the west of London on the Thames, will delight gardeners: Hampton Court Palace and Kew Gardens. Hampton Court was built in 1514 by the Archbishop of York – until King Henry VIII liked what he saw and took it for himself. It was opened to the public by Queen Victoria. Kew Gardens is one of the world's greatest botanical gardens and is a World Heritage site.

MANCHESTER

The capital of northern England in everything but name, Manchester is a vibrant, engaging city that has played a central part in British sport and music in recent decades. Several new projects, sparked by the Commonwealth Games which the city hosted in 2002, have increased its appeal as a short break destination. Chief among these world-class attractions is Urbis, a contemporary, glass-walled exhibition centre dedicated to showing new work in art, design, architecture and music. Interaction is part of many of the exhibitions and the centre is aimed at visitors of all ages.

Art lovers should head for the newly-redeveloped Salford Quays where the shimmering steel structure of the Lowry has won architecture awards. LS Lowry was a Mancunian artist best known for the evocative, industrial landscapes he painted and the stick figures he peopled them with. The Lowry has a permanent exhibition of his work plus visiting exhibitions from contemporary artists. There is also a theatre in the complex that stages concerts, comedians and shows.

The northern branch of the excellent Imperial War Museum is also in Salford Quays and is housed in a similarly bold building, resembling three shards of steel. The Castlefield area of Manchester is known for its nightlife with bars owned by musicians and footballers. Anyone with an interest in football will be aware of Manchester

United's Old Trafford ground, but the city is also the base for Britain's gold medal-winning track cycling squad and the Manchester Velodrome offers an exciting night out watching the cyclists during the winter season.

Manchester's Rival, Liverpool

Home to four Beatles, two cathedrals and a very famous river, Liverpool is just 48 kilometres (30 miles) away from Manchester and makes for an interesting day out. Many Beatles fans make the pilgrimage to Liverpool to see the original Strawberry Fields, Penny Lane and the childhood homes of John Lennon and Paul McCartney, both now owned by the National Trust and open to the public. Two museums at the Albert Dock, on the Mersey River, have more Beatles memorabilia.

HOW TO GET THERE
Manchester airport receives flights from several European airlines including Scandinavian Airlines, Air France, Iberia and Lufthansa.

CONTACTS/FURTHER INFORMATION
www.visitmanchester.com
www.urbis.org.uk
www.thelowry.com

A Manchester canal

101

NEWQUAY

HOW TO GET THERE
Ryanair flies to Newquay from London Stansted. The train operator First Great Western has express services into Cornwall from London and other parts of the UK.

CONTACTS/FURTHER INFORMATION
www.visitsouthwest.co.uk
www.edenproject.com

Biomes at the Eden Project

You don't have to pack a surfboard for a weekend in Newquay, England's premier surf spot; there are plenty to rent, as well as surf schools, on the town's main beach, Fistral. But if you're not a surfer or the swell is flat, there's plenty to do in the region.

Newquay sits on the north coast of Cornwall, a county that has provided childhood holiday memories for whole generations of Britons. This southwest tip of England is where life (and sometimes the traffic) slows to a leisurely pace. The rugged beaches are part of Cornwall's appeal and you can walk from one to another along the South West Coast Path, which runs along the fractured Cornish coastline. Sun seekers will want to come in the summer months when the sea is almost warm enough to swim in while surfers prefer the stormier autumn and winter months for the larger waves: wetsuits would be required.

Away from the beaches, Cornwall might seem like a quaint land of cream tea shops and dry stone walling, but there are pockets of sophistication. North of Newquay, the dining options in Padstow are as good as any in London. Celebrity chefs Jamie Oliver and Rick Stein have transformed the town into a foodie haven to mixed reaction from the locals. Continue up the north coast for the moody Tintagel Castle, a 13th century ruin clinging to the cliffs.

On the south coast of Cornwall, the Eden Project is a nationally renowned eco-project. A series of biomes, like giant, transparent golf balls sunk into a quarry, recreate ecosystems and climates from around the world, from the Amazon to California. It's a fascinating day out and there is usually something extra going on during the school holidays. On the other side of St. Austell from the Eden Project, the Lost Gardens of Heligan makes a less high-tech but just as enthralling journey into the world of horticulture. Restormel Castle, nearby, is a rare example of an intact Norman castle.